Risk Reward

RISK REWARD

The Art and Science of Successful Trading

Howard Abell

Great Lakes College
Midland

Dearborn
Financial Publishing, Inc.®

Editorial Director: Cynthia A. Zigmund
Managing Editor: Jack Kiburz
Project Editor: Trey Thoelcke
Interior Design: Lucy Jenkins
Cover Design: Scott Rattray Design
Cover Photo Courtesy of the Chicago Board of Trade

© 1998 by Innergame Partners

Published by Dearborn Financial Publishing, Inc.®

Printed in the United States of America

98 99 00 10 9 8 7 6 5 4 3 2 1

Library of Congress Cataloging-in-Publication Data

Abell, Howard
    Risk reward : the art and science of successful trading / Howard Abell.
        p.   cm.
    Includes bibliographical references (p.   ).
    ISBN 0-7931-2663-0 (hardcover)
    1. Futures–United States.   2. Speculation–United States.
3. Stockbrokers–United States–Psychology.   4. Investment analysis.
I. Title.
HG6024.U6A627 1998
332.63'228–dc21   98-21904
                                                                CIP

Dearborn books are available at special quantity discounts to use as premiums and sales promotions, or for use in corporate training programs. For more information, please call the Special Sales Manager at 800-621-9621, ext. 4384, or write to Dearborn Financial Publishing, Inc., 155 North Wacker Drive, Chicago, IL 60606-1719.

Dedication

This book is dedicated to all traders who face risk.
It is this constant that links each of us to one another.

Contents

Foreword

To many, *risk* is a four-letter word. For Howard Abell, his new book *Risk Reward: The Art and Science of Successful Trading* marks the continuation of a thoughtful quest to understand the quixotic psyche of the professional trader. Metaphorically speaking, Howard continues like a cross between Jason and Diogenes in search of discovering the "secret" of how professional traders create wealth from markets.

Risk Reward discusses the academic side of probability and statistics and proceeds to explore how practitioners use this science to construct successful trading careers. The scientific concepts explored herein were taught to me in school so long ago that I forgot the learning of them, but in fact had internalized them into a coherent set of practices that worked for me. In that sense *Risk Reward* resonates perfectly with me. As I read, I kept saying "Aha, I remember this!"

Now you are probably saying, "Okay Jeff, quit fencing about the edges, come clean—tell us exactly how you use the concepts contained in *Risk Reward* to make big money in the financial and commodities markets." So here it is: Markets can only go up or down. Success comes from doing several things very well, such as

- Picking the market direction correctly
- Timing the entry and exit of the trade precisely
- Avoiding what money management rules call the "risk of ruin"
- Tolerating what I call "noise," as in signal-to-noise ratio (what Warren Buffett refers to as "quotational risk")
- Avoiding the emotional content of decisions, yet using internal stimuli to guide decision making

That's all there is. But it's not so simple! To succeed at trading you need to be simultaneously humble and superconfident—humble enough to admit you are wrong, humble enough to take personal responsibility for everything that goes awry. Yet you must have the confidence and temperament to take on the world and say, in effect, "All of you are wrong—I am right!" Believe me, there is a lot of self-analysis, experience (much of it painful and costly), and soul searching that goes into resolving this paradox.

In trading one learns that risk and reward are opposite sides of the same coin. In this world, you only get paid for providing a service. Selectively carrying risk is a service that can pay very, very well, thank you!

Risk can be addictive, sorry to say. It seems to me that many professional traders get hooked on a level of excitement and risk in their lives. That risk must be sufficient to achieve the adrenaline rush, so they tend to trade bigger and bigger in rough proportion to their bankroll and consideration of the increasing lack of liquidity for larger positions. This is somewhat contrary to the scientific concepts of risk determined by studying people in games of chance. Additionally, there is a behavior psychology component to traders' addictions. Gamblers and losing traders are typically hooked even stronger than successful traders by virtue of the intermittent nature of the reward. My cat follows me into the kitchen every time I go, yet not one in ten times does he get his turkey snack reward! I suspect that this behavior is practically impossible to extinguish.

To achieve success in a game that many try and most lose is quite a challenge. The task of acquiring knowledge about markets and about oneself is both difficult and rewarding. Trading has been, and always will be, "A hard way to make an easy living!" Understanding the concepts discussed in *Risk Reward: The Art and Science of Successful Trading* makes the process just a little less difficult and a lot more rewarding!

—Jeffrey Silverman
Director, Chicago Mercantile Exchange

Preface

The concept of risk is central to any comprehensive understanding of markets and individual trading performance. When to embrace risk rather than to avoid it and how to circumscribe risk rather than allowing it to get out of control are issues that need to be scrupulously addressed in order to trade markets effectively.

In his book *The Psychology of Technical Analysis,* Tony Plummer very succinctly stated the critical dilemma facing the trader at the moment of decision making.

> The question for the trader is whether it really is possible to divorce the longer-term goal of profitable trading from the potentially traumatic short-term effects of incurring losses. The answer lies in the making of two specific commitments. The first is the commitment to use a technical trading system which provides automatic entry and exit criteria and which incorporates money management principles. . . . The second commitment is the adoption of an attitude toward oneself which is supportive of trading.

I believe a thorough understanding of risk from both a historical and operational perspective provides the trader a very useful lens with which to view the markets in order to adopt profitable trading strategies and management tactics.

To the best of my knowledge, nowhere in the literature has anyone fully analyzed the psychological concept of risk in the invariable daily context in which professional traders make their decisions: inconclusive and conflicting market information, debilitating human emotions, and faulty technical indicators that lack certainty. Probing the concept of risk provides us with a much better understanding of the internal concerns facing the individual trader (i.e., confidence, consistency, individual certainty) as well as a more dynamic understanding of the market as a whole (i.e., herd psychology, market value, etc.).

The goal of *Risk Reward* is to vigorously explore the concept of risk in terms of its many applications in order to optimize individual trader performance. I am exploring how we perceive risk, how we as individuals avoid or embrace it. It is, after all, our perception of risk that determines the actions we take in the markets or in our daily lives. It is this perception, in the final analysis, that determines whether we step tentatively off the curb, looking nervously both ways into traffic, or choose to stride brazenly across a tightrope 300 feet above the ground. This will be accomplished through a philosophical and psychological discussion of risk in all its complexity, as well as through identifying the subtle ways risk can be managed and controlled to maximize investment opportunities. Moreover, the interviews with experts and top traders will demonstrate the challenges and opportunities that risk presents.

Risk Reward builds logically on my previous books, *The Innergame of Trading, The Outer Game of Trading, The Day Trader's Advantage,* and *Spread Trading,* and represents a significant contribution to the literature in order to better understand markets and individual trader performance.

Acknowledgments

I wish to acknowledge the many contributors to *Risk Reward* who gave generously of their time, despite demanding schedules. Their candor and insights into the workings of their minds provide a rare glimpse into the way professional traders calculate, manage, and ultimately control the daily risk that each must face. They are: Larry Carr, Toby Crabel, Scott Foster, Tom Grossman, Charles LeBeau, Larry Rosenberg, David Silverman, and Jeffrey Silverman.

In particular I would like to thank my friend and business partner Bob Koppel for his expert advice and guidance.

I also want to thank Cynthia Zigmund and the entire staff at Dearborn Financial Publishing. This is the third book I have written for Dearborn; their ongoing commitment to excellence and their enthusiasm for this project are once again kindly acknowledged.

The trader is like a Masai Warrior who each day must "face the knife" and hunt the lion with only spear and bare hands. His success will come from relying on his own wits and instincts at the moment of truth, embracing risk as his ally to achieve the desired outcome.

—Robert Koppel, *The Tao of Trading*

1

The History of Risk

My life was a risk I had to take.
—Bertrand Russell

Evidence of risk taking, mostly in the form of games of chance, has been noted in history as far back as recorded time. Throwing dice made of animal bones, drawing lots, and playing card games are described in stories from the Bible and depicted in drawings from ancient Greece, as well as in the Asian fortune-telling cards that are the forerunners of modern card games.

Of course, games of chance must be distinguished from games of skill in which specific modes of thought and behavior directly influence the outcome. In gambling, time is the dominant factor. In essence, risk and time are opposite sides of the same coin. In his groundbreaking work on risk, *Against the Gods: The Remarkable Story of Risk,* Peter Bernstein writes, "Time transforms risk, and the nature of risk is shaped by the time horizon: the future is the playing field."

The ancient Greeks with their skill as mathematicians and logicians had the tools to found and implement probability theory, but the Greeks had little interest in advancing the cause of managing

1

the future. In fact, the prevailing attitude then and for centuries afterwards was that the future was a matter of luck or random happenstance and that decision making was driven by instinct.

When the Crusaders opened the door to the Arab world, it soon became apparent that the Arabs were at a higher intellectual level than the Christians in terms of science and mathematics. The Arabs incorporated the Hindu numbering system into their high-level scientific research and experimentation. The new numbering system that replaced the abacus and movable counters evolved into written methods of computation. As a result, over the next 500 years, great strides were made in abstract mathematical thinking, travel, time keeping, architectural construction, and production methods. However, not until the Renaissance and the Protestant Reformation did science and logic gain a solid foothold and people begin to realize that they were not at the mercy of the gods or random chance.

Trade blossomed. Exploring the new world and accumulating wealth invited the adventuresome: risk takers, explorers, and businessmen. These new activities demanded new skills and new thinking. Bookkeeping created the need for new numbering and counting techniques. Thinking about the future and forecasting unforeseen outcomes became a new reality.

Along with trade, the Renaissance produced the highest level of intellectual activity in science, the arts, mathematics, and architecture. Girolamo Cardano was a sixteenth-century physician and mathematical thinker with a taste for gambling. His treatise on gambling, titled *Liber de Ludo Aleae (Book on Games of Chance)*, was one of the earliest attempts at developing the statistical principles of probability.

Throughout Europe, interest in and ideas about probability and risk were gaining enthusiasm. Bernstein notes,

France in particular was the scene of a veritable explosion of mathematical innovation during the seventeenth and eighteenth centuries that went far beyond Cardano's empirical dice-tossing experiments. Advances in calculus and algebra led to increasingly abstract concepts that provided the foundation for many practical applications of probability, from insurance and investment to such far-distant subjects as medicine, heredity, the behavior of molecules, the conduct of war, and weather forecasting.

The intellectual curiosity and power of three French men gave us a leap forward in probability theory: Blaise Pascal was a celebrated mathematician and philosopher; Chevalier de Mere, a skilled mathematician; and Pierre de Fermat, a lawyer with a rare gift for mathematics.

Chevalier de Mere introduced Pascal to Luca Paccioli's old brain teaser—how should two players in a game of *balla* share the stakes when they leave the game uncompleted? It had not been solved up to that point. Pascal approached Fermat with the problem and began a long-term correspondence that resulted in significant contributions to the theory of probability.

Not until 1738 were risk taking and human behavior understood to be two halves of a complex, mutually interactive whole, as they are known to be today. A Swiss mathematician named Daniel Bernoulli published an essay exploring the idea that people making choices consider not only outcomes but also the consequences of each possible outcome. This was a major change in the mathematicians' world of numbers, probabilities, and outcomes. It introduced the notion that people view the consequences of their decisions not only in terms of actual numbers but in what these numbers or outcomes are worth to them in psychological terms. We have come to know this as "the utility of an outcome." The utility value of an outcome is different for each person making a decision when the future is uncertain. In other words, we all look at risk differently; risks and the outcomes of those risks mean different things to each of us. Bernoulli theorized that the value a person puts on an outcome is inversely related to what that person already owns.

Bernoulli included the motivations of the person who assumes the risk, an entirely new direction in the study of probability and risk that afforded exciting implications for how people make choices in all areas of their lives. Of course, this new line of thinking also explains in part why valuations in tulips and stocks can approach distorted levels, even for a short time. It also suggests why under certain circumstances a small chance of a large gain is more inviting than the certainty of a very small gain.

Risk: Science or Art?

Risk, whether welcome or unwelcome, is an integral part of our lives. Successful living demands choices and choices create risk. The inherent nature of choice is uncertainty, and with uncertainty comes risk. We make choices that we hope will reduce or eliminate risk only to find that we have created other risks in its place. We may avoid risk by staying close to home, only to discover that the greatest risk of accident is right there. We may move away from the city to escape crime and pollution, only to realize that medical services are dangerously far away. We may invest personal financial assets in "safe" government securities, only to have inflation strip away their value. We may even think that by refusing to make a choice we can avoid risk, but that too is a delusion. The only time there is no risk is when there is no choice.

There are, however, circumstances where we create a risk for ourselves where none would exist. If we are contemplating the purchase of stock in a company, that purchase can have two outcomes. The stock may go up in value, thereby giving us a gain, or it may decline in value, resulting in a loss. Our other option is to do nothing, which in this case does not affect our bottom line at all. In effect, our choices are the status quo of not purchasing the stock or the risk of purchase that could lead to a profit or a loss.

We could add another level to this process—by taking no action, we also lose the opportunity to gain from that purchase. We can identify a risky situation by several inherent factors. The first, of course, is an unknown outcome. If outcome is predetermined or known in advance there can be no risk. The second is lack of complete control to affect the outcome. If we could completely control a situation we would give ourselves the best outcome. Another is lack of all information available. If we had all the information, or for that matter knew what the end result of an action or event would be, we would choose the best alternative. And finally, the element of time. We must make a decision before the facts of a risky situation or event unfold. We would love the luxury of time to evaluate the eventual outcome or even wait until it becomes clear what the result would be before making the appropriate choice.

Risk Behavior

We have discussed how risky situations involve alternatives or choices. To me, the most interesting aspects of risk taking are how people perceive risk and risky situations and how they respond to these choices. There are many alternatives in a risky situation, and different people deal with these alternatives in different ways. There are a range of responses from risk averseness to risk taking and everything in between.

Of course, before we take on risk we must study the alternatives available in a risky situation. Some are obvious, as when two alternatives will result in the same outcome but one will result in a greater loss. But what about when one alternative will result in a larger positive outcome but also may result in a greater loss, while the other alternative will yield a smaller gain but also a smaller loss? What if one alternative's chance of success was less than another's but would yield a greater gain? How do you choose if one alternative has a high probability of success for a small gain while another has a small probability of success for a huge gain?

In studying risk behavior we must look into how people recognize risk, how they perceive the risks they recognize, and how they evaluate the risks they perceive.

Recognition

Dealing with risks requires that we recognize risk when we see it. Most people recognize a risk if they perceive that a situation may result in a loss of any kind. Even if an impartial observer "sees" the risk differently, it's the decision maker's perception that's important. At a cocktail party one evening I overheard someone ask a successful commodities trader if trading was too risky. He replied, "Not when I do it!" We learn about risk from past experiences or our individual skills. If you're an experienced alligator wrestler, you may not understand why others shy away.

We usually focus on monetary losses but there are other types of losses that either accompany monetary loss or are separate. A risky situation may result in the loss of face, self-esteem, prestige, authority, or reputation. Concern for these other potential outcomes, along with monetary loss, complicates how each person perceives and reacts to a risky situation.

Evaluation

After entering into or finding oneself in a risky situation, the person must evaluate whether he or she wants to stay in or to get out. If the risks are found to be unacceptable, the person can abandon the situation. If, on the other hand, the choice is to stay in the "opportunity," then a new series of evaluations must continue to take place as the situation unfolds.

Adjusting to Risk

Risk can be embraced either in a passive or active manner. In most instances we have continuous choices about reducing the chance of loss, or the magnitude of the loss, or our general exposure. Passive involvement requires us to adopt a course of action and see it through to the end. It means a single choice. Many people are more willing to take an active role in trying to adjust the various components of a risk situation. If possible they may take steps to reduce their exposure or modify any one of a number of alternatives available to them. They may try to find ways to gain time or information or attempt to gain greater control over the situation. Usually there are tradeoffs when attempting to manipulate the components of risk. If we modify our exposure it may also modify the potential gain. If we somehow buy time it may increase our maximum loss.

• • • • • • • • •

From the Greeks to about the time of Bernoulli, the focus on risk had been to quantify and measure probabilities. Bernoulli opened a small crack in the door when he introduced the concept of utility. No matter how rational an idea or what measurement of probability one uses, people end up making decisions based as much or more on personal preferences and emotional arguments as pure mathematics.

From these beginnings and the gradual introduction of the concept of loss, we came to realize that Bernoulli's utility theory was inadequate to explain people's behavior in the face of uncertainty. However, until the middle of the twentieth century the emphasis was still placed on measuring and defining risk in almost purely mathematical terms.

Three things occurred that widened the crack in the door opened up by Bernoulli. The first was the invention of game theory by John von Neumann, a physicist. Although game theory emphasizes that the winner will always be the player who behaves the most rationally according to the constraints laid down by the game rules, it also introduced the idea that alternatives were not set in stone but were constantly shifting along with the wants and desires of other players.

In essence, game theory brought a new meaning to the concept of uncertainty. Earlier theories accepted uncertainty as a fact of life and did little to identify its source. Game theory proposed that *the true source of uncertainty lies in the intentions of others.*

From this perspective, almost every decision we make is the result of a series of negotiations in which we try to reduce uncertainty by trading off what other people want in return for what we want ourselves. Like poker and chess, real life is a game of strategy, with contracts and handshakes to protect us from cheaters.

Unlike in poker and chess, we can seldom expect to be an absolute declared "winner" in these games. Choosing the alternative that we judge will bring us the highest payoff tends to be the riskiest decision, because it may provoke the strongest defense from players who stand to lose if we have our way. To make the best of a bad bargain, game theory uses terms like *maximin* and *minimax* to describe such decisions. Think of terms such as *seller-buyer, landlord-tenant, husband-wife, lender-borrower.*

In the late 1930s, von Neumann met the German-born economist Oskar Morgenstern. The two collaborated for many years and the result was *Theory of Game and Economic Behavior.* This classic work combined game theory and its application to decision making in areas such as economics and business.

In 1952, an article appeared in the *Journal of Finance* titled "Portfolio Selection." It was an academic study involving equity investments and risk. The author was Harry Markowitz, a graduate student at the University of Chicago, whose work proved so profound that he received a Nobel Prize in economics.

Markowitz linked the notion of expected rate of return to something he called variance. Although Markowitz doesn't use the word *risk,* variance and risk have become interchangeable. What Markowitz says is that the variance or standard deviation is the swing of the average return above or below it. It was the first time anyone had qualified the rate of return of an investment. In other words, it is just as important in creating an investment portfolio to determine to what extent that portfolio will move up and down before coming to rest at a desired rate of return. Let's say that an investment could deliver a rate of return of 10 percent per year but the variance or standard deviation of that investment was 15 percent. This would mean that two-thirds of the return would fall between 10 percent plus 15 percent, or 25 percent on the upside, and 10 percent minus 15 percent, or minus 5 percent on the downside.

The use of diversification is how Markowitz controlled variance. The most desirable outcome is the highest rate of return possible with the lowest risk necessary to achieve that rate of return. By creating a "portfolio," an investment with many parts, you rule out the chance of making a killing but also the probability of getting financially killed. Essentially, the rate of return of your investment will be the average rate of return of all the individual pieces of that investment. The volatility or variance will be less than the average volatility of the individual pieces.

So by selecting a combination of securities that range from staid to risky and by keeping the correlation of those securities as low as possible, you may be able to achieve a rate of return higher than if you were restricted to all high-grade securities. For example, studies have shown that a portfolio of stocks and bonds may be enhanced by the inclusion of managed futures. These studies have shown that at any particular rate of return the variance is lower than for a portfolio of only stocks and bonds at the same rate of return.

It is now common practice in every area of the investment community to diversify. Portfolio managers not only diversify stocks and industries but countries and continents as well. Emerging markets, for example, can be an integral part of a conservative portfolio, although its volatility would preclude its use as a stand-alone investment.

All of this doesn't come easy. Making sure that the individual pieces of a portfolio have the lowest covariance or correlation is a requirement of success. However, a device was created by William Sharpe, a colleague of Markowitz's who shared the Nobel Prize with him. In its simplest terms, this device compares the volatility of individual stocks, or any other asset for that matter, with the market as a whole over some period. This relationship is called the beta of an investment. For example, IBM might have a beta of 1.25, which means that it would tend to move up or down 1.25 percent each time the S&P 500 moved up or down 1 percent.

However, like everything else in life, you can't set up risk and its determinants in black and white. People have different attitudes about what is risky and what is not. We have come a long way since Pascal, Fermat, and Bernoulli, all of whom based their ideas in mathematical certainties and a belief that rational decision making could be ordained by strict adherence to the probabilistic formulas derived.

People are too complicated to be put into a box labeled Rational Decisions. Ideas about risk and desirable outcomes are as diverse as people themselves. In the last several years there has been more evidence that inconsistencies in rational decision making could be part of a natural pattern of behavior. That is to say, we might not really know what rational behavior really is or should be.

This is essentially where research on risk has been going for the past two decades. The most prominent of this research was conducted by two Israeli psychologists, Daniel Kahneman and Amos Tversky.

In March of 1979, Kahneman and Tversky published "Prospect Theory: An Analysis of Decision Under Risk," in the journal *Econometrica.* Their work found behavior that wasn't sustained by previous research in rational decision making. They introduced emotion, which often overwhelms the self-control necessary to make rational decisions. They came to realize that people do not have the ability to completely understand the problems they are dealing with. Psychologists call this cognitive difficulty. One of the most interesting findings of the prospect theory is the way that people make decisions involving gains and losses. They found that if people are given a choice between a certain gain and a fair gamble for a larger gain, they will take the certain gain. A simple demonstration of this phenomenon follows.

> Subjects were given the choice of an 80 percent chance of 4,000 versus a certain 3,000. Mathematically, the expectation of the choice of 4,000 is worth 3,200, yet 80 percent of the subjects chose the certain 3,000. These people were risk averse.

But then the problem was turned around and presented as follows.

> Subjects were given the choice of an 80 percent chance of losing 4,000 versus a certain loss of 3,000. The mathematical expectation of choosing the 4,000 loss is 3,200 versus the 3,000, yet 92 percent of the subjects chose to take the gamble. When the choice involved taking a loss, people became risk takers.

Tversky concluded that loss aversion is the primary driving force.

In their article "Judgment under Uncertainty: Heuristics and Biases," Tversky and Kahneman state,

> The subjective assessment of probability resembles the subjective assessment of physical quantities such as distance or size. These judgments are all based on data of limited validity, which are processed according to heuristic rules. For example, the apparent distance of an object is determined in part by its clarity. The more sharply the object is seen, the closer it

appears to be. This rule has some validity, because in any given scene the more distant objects are seen less sharply than nearer objects. However, the reliance on this rule leads to systematic errors in the estimation of distance. Specifically, distances are often overestimated when visibility is poor because the contours of objects are blurred. On the other hand, distances are often underestimated when visibility is good because the objects are seen sharply. Thus, the reliance on clarity as an indication of distance leads to common biases. Such biases are also found in the intuitive judgment of probability.

All this seems to be saying that notwithstanding all of the mathematical models, the law of probability, game theory, and rational people making rational decisions, we are apt to fly by the seat of our pants when assessing risk. In fact, we may take it one step further and theorize that rational decision making is the exception and judgment by emotion and imperfect reasoning is the norm.

In his book *The Intuitive Trader,* Robert Koppel writes,

Successful trading—that is, consistently profitable trading—involves far more than merely calling upon specific mechanical and strategic skills. It requires the development, cultivation, and conditioning of habits, thought patterns, and attitudes that influence the way we think and behave in the market. The toughest part of trading, in my view, is to overcome the rigid intellectual guardianship of the left brain, which serves to habituate existing behaviors and to rationalize the need for "logical consistency," and thus to emancipate the intuitive right side of our brain, the key to changing ingrained thought patterns and habits.

We all recognize that the notion of real life investors being able to accurately and consistently make trades free of any emotion is challenging to say the least. For most of us our emotions are too involved in our decision-making process to allow us to adhere purely to some mathematical model.

Is there an investor out there who has not agonized over the decision to sell, buy, or buy back after selling out? To most of us these decisions are contingent on many psychological factors that add a high degree of complexity to an ability to take on and manage risk.

Let us now turn to the specific psychological and strategic aspects of risk taking that will allow us to maximize our trading and investment opportunities.

2

The Psychology
of Risk

*There is no way you can compare someone who
takes financial risks to what I did....
The line is as wide as the Snake River Canyon....
If you haven't played Russian Roulette
you can't understand!*

—*Evel Knievel*

Why is it that one person very tentatively crosses a city street,
looking both ways, exhibiting anxiety and trepidation, while another strings a wire across the twin towers of the World Trade Cen-
ter and cavalierly prances to and fro in 20-knot winds? Why is it that
even though modern mathematics and probability theory have
proven that flying in an airplane is statistically safer by tenfold than
driving in a car, we gladly hand over our car keys to our sixteen-
year-olds yet experience anxiety when flying on an airplane? Why
is it that some of us trade easily in financial and commodity options
and futures while others invest in government securities? In short,
why is it that some people perceive risk where others see none?

In *The Innergame of Trading* and *The Outer Game of Trading,* Bob Koppel and I explored the emotional and psychological
barriers that are an integral part of success or failure in trading.
Specifically, we identified the importance of particular psychological skills that are necessary in order to become a successful
trader. These skills are as essential to the long-term equities

15

trader or investor as they are to the short-term commodities option or futures trader.

The list below lists the specific psychological skills necessary to becoming a successful trader or investor.

- Compelling Personal Motivation
- Goal Setting
- Confidence
- Anxiety Control
- Focus
- State Management

Compelling Personal Motivation

Compelling motivation is possessing the intensity to do whatever it takes to win at trading; to overcome a bad day or setback in order to achieve your trading goals. Think of the intensity of a world-class athlete: fully engaged and not afraid to play the game, not afraid of "being there," totally involved in the moment.

In order for a trading strategy to be successful, it must incorporate all the psychological, technical, and financial resources that are at your disposal. The difficulty with most trading strategies is that they don't adequately deal with the central issue of trading, namely, taking a loss. In my experience most traders deal with the issue of loss in a variety of maladaptive ways, the most common of which are the following:

- Denial
- Inaction
- Confusion
- Anger

There is another aspect of taking a loss that is rarely addressed in books on trading—the psychological and emotional responses that inhibit the development and implementation of an effective trading strategy. Learning to take a loss is the single hardest lesson a trader has to learn. Truly learning how to take a loss will allow the trader to maintain a compelling personal motivation. The following lists describe how traders respond to loss.

Physical Symptoms of Taking a Loss

- Rapid or shallow breathing
- Sweating
- Constriction of muscles
- Upset stomach
- Tension
- Feelings of malaise

Emotional Symptoms of Taking a Loss

- Anger
- Depression
- Disillusionment
- Distraction
- General anxiety
- Irritability
- Frustration
- Low self-worth
- Embarrassment

Visual Imagery Traders Process Internally When Taking a Loss

- Sights of past failures
- Pictures of trading obstacles and disappointments
- Visions of unrelated mishaps of a general nature

Auditory Imagery Traders Process Internally When Taking a Loss

- The voice of doom and failure
- Replaying negative experiences from the past
- Remembering why you are "so incompetent"

Bodily Imagery Traders Experience When Taking a Loss

- Body feels heavy
- Shoulders drop
- Torso is hunched
- Facial muscles slacken
- Breathing is short and shallow
- Eyes are cast down
- Trader feels slow, weak, or out of energy

Anxiety Traders Experience Relating to Loss

- Fear of failure
- Fear of success
- Fear of inadequacy
- Loss of control

Thoughts Traders Have When Taking a Loss

- "I don't know what I'm doing."
- "These markets are impossible."
- "I'm too small, inexperienced, young, old, etc."
- "I don't have a clear strategy."
- "What will X think of me?"
- "I'm a loser, fool, incompetent, etc."

Beliefs Traders Possess about Themselves and the Market When Taking a Loss

About the market

- "The market is rigged."
- "It's impossible to have a winning trade."
- "You can never get a decent fill."

About themselves

- "I can never make a winning trade."
- "I have to be perfect."
- "If I take a loss, then I'm a loser."
- "I'm just too afraid to take the risk."

Self-Defeating Attitudes That Traders Possess When Taking a Loss

- Trying to please others
- Thinking in absolute terms
- Focusing on negative things
- Demanding certainty or "absolute" control
- Defining trading as impossible

- Representing a bad trade as a catastrophe
- Not understanding that it is risk that allows for opportunity

Goal Setting

Goal setting is imperative to the trader, not only in terms of setting realistic and measurable goals within the context of a specific time frame but also in terms of enhancing motivation and performance. Setting goals, in fact, conditions the trader on an ongoing basis to boost his trading to the next level. It is excellence, not perfection, that is the point here. The list that follows describes the importance of setting goals.

Goal Setting

- Identifies what is important to you
- Increases your motivation
- Directs your focus
- Identifies relevant trading strategies

Identifying what is important to you. Trading goals help put things into perspective. They provide direction and point you toward your intended outcome by the quickest route.

Increasing motivation. You can only reach your full potential as a trader if your motivation and effort are high. Goals provide for a continuing and energized attitude. Keeping your goal in the forefront of your mind motivates you to work harder, give more effort (physically and emotionally), and keep striving to improve.

Directing your focus. Goals direct your attitude to specifically accomplish those patterns of thought and behavior that will allow you to become disciplined, confident, and consistent.

Identifying relevant trading strategies. Your goal allows you to identify the overall strategy and those specific techniques that will allow you to accomplish your trading objectives.

FIGURE 2.1 The Importance of Trading Goals

Goal	Benefit	Trading Behavior
Performance Goal	Focus on improvement in relation to your own standards.	Increases physical and psychological skills related to trading.
Outcome Goal	Helps determine what's important to you.	Allows for the development of techniques and strategies that match your personality.
Motivation Goal	Helps increase effort and direct attention.	Allows traders to maintain a high level of enthusiasm and confidence.

FIGURE 2.2 Operational Definition of Trading Goals

Specific	Clear, precise, well-defined.
Time-framed	State within a specific time period.
Positive	State it in a way that is empowering.
Control	It should be completely within your control.
Realistic	Making a million on your first trade does not satisfy our definition.
Measurable	Easily quantifiable.

FIGURE 2.3   Monthly Goal Chart

My long-term goal is _____.

My goal for this month is _____.

My goal for this week is _____.

My strategy for achieving these goals is _____.

The Factors That Prevent Traders from Achieving Their Trading Goals

- Self-limiting beliefs
- Unresourceful state
- Poor focus
- Ill-defined personal strategy
- Lack of physical and psychological energy

Self-limiting beliefs.   Inhibiting beliefs about oneself and the market. Examples of such beliefs are:

- "I'm uncertain."
- "I don't believe in myself."
- "How can I be sure?"
- "How do I know I won't get a terrible fill?"
- "How can I compete with the locals?"

Unresourceful state.   An unresourceful state is when the predominant emotions a trader is experiencing are anxiety, confusion, and/or fear. Traders report

- "I'm angry."
- "All I feel is frustration."
- "I'm just afraid to pull the trigger."

- "I just close my eyes and pray."
- "I want revenge."

Poor focus. Poor focus is when trades are made as a result of distracted concentration, when a trader's point of focus is not crystal clear, laser-straight. They report

- "All I can think of is the last loss."
- "Those bad fills keep getting in my way."
- "Why do I always get head-faked?"
- "I can't see the forest for the trees."
- "I'm always distracted just at the point of decision."

Ill-defined personal strategy. An ill-defined personal strategy is characterized by trades that are made with a high level of emotional content; trading becomes little more than an impulse response to one's personal state. Traders who have experienced this report

- "I'm trading by the seat of my pants."
- "I don't have a clear plan."
- "My methodology is no more than a collection of tactics."
- "Sometimes it works and sometimes it doesn't."

Lack of physical and psychological energy. Lack of physical and psychological energy result from one's anxiety level. One experiences tension and resulting physical and psychological fatigue. Traders have told us

- "I just feel totally wiped."
- "I'm a psychological zombie."
- "I don't have enough energy to trade."

Goal Setting Guidelines

Learning to set realistic but challenging goals is not a mystical process. What follow here are five specific steps to take to reach your trading goals.

1. Identify your goals.
   - What are your trading goals?
   - What do you want to accomplish?
   - What is your long-term goal?
   - What is your short-term goal?
   - Why is it important for you to achieve these goals?
   - What is preventing you from achieving your goal right now?
   - What specific actions or steps can you take to achieve your goals today?
   - What are your greatest weaknesses as a trader?
   - What do you find most interesting about trading?
   - How much effort, time, and money are you willing to commit to trading?
   - Is it important for you to trade by feel?
   - Is it important for you to have a totally mechanical system?
   - What does the ideal trading system look like to you?
2. Set challenging goals.
   - Do you prepare mentally for trading?
   - Are you physically prepared? (I'm not joking)
   - Do you understand the strategic aspects of trading effectively?
   - Are your mechanical skills well-honed?
3. Set specific measurable goals and target dates.
4. Set performance goals for motivation, outcome goals to identify the big picture.
5. Find success in everything you do.

In *The Mental Game,* James Loehr makes this point as it relates to tennis. I believe it applies equally well to trading.

If losing is equated with failure, the battle of confidence cannot be won. Your motto should always be, "Win or lose, another step forward." You can find success in a losing effort when you establish clear performance goals prior to the match. You have the potential to learn much more from a loss than a victory. When you set your goals properly, your confidence can continue to grow, independent of your match's outcome.

Confidence

Confidence based on competence is purely a result of motivation, belief (in oneself and the market), and state of mind. Confidence in psychological terms is no more than consistently expecting a positive outcome. Think of anything you have ever done in your life with that feeling of confidence (positive expectation). Did not that feeling ultimately predict a successful result? It is the same with trading.

Anxiety Control

The trader must learn how to overcome the following anxieties:

- Fear of failure—Trader feels intense pressure to perform and ties self-worth to trading.
- Fear of success—Trader loses control; euphoric trading and self-doubt.
- Fear of inadequacy—Trader experiences loss of self-esteem, diminished confidence.
- Loss of control—Trader loses sense of personal responsibility when trading; feels market is out to get him.

Focus

The tighter your focus and the finer the distinctions you bring to your trading focus, the better the results will be. Focus is one of those terms that sounds like a cliché unless you understand how to utilize it in your trading. It is through focus that one stays consistent and is able to maintain a high level of confidence. Focus derives from developing a specific strategy that allows you to feel certain and act accordingly.

State Management

FIGURE 2.4   The Syntax of Successful Trading

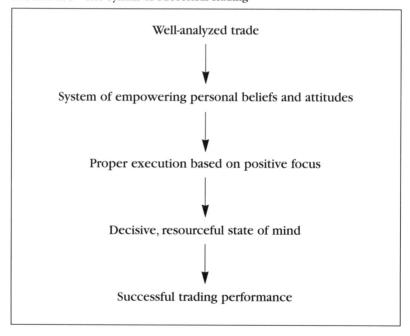

How you feel at any given moment in time will determine your state of mind, including what you feel physically, represent visually, and process emotionally about your trading. Learning how to manage your state will determine whether you hesitate or act and whether you are emotionally drained or physically and psychologically energized. Figure 2.5 summarizes successful trading performance in terms of what we see, hear, and feel.

FIGURE 2.5 Successful Trading Performance

Bodily Response	Visualization	Auditory
Body feels light, shoulders are erect, torso is straight. Facial muscles are taut, breathing is deep and relaxed. Eyes look up and straight ahead. Trader is feeling strong, energized, and enthusiastic.	Seeing yourself succeed. Watching yourself in control, relaxed, looking competent, confident, and positive.	The voice of confidence and control. The sound of relaxed, effortless trading.

Positive Imagery

We have the power and ability to choose what imagery we process in our minds and bodies. We can literally choose the character and intensity of the images (feeling on a physical level) that are of a visual, auditory, and kinesthetic (physical) nature. We can see failure or success, trading loss or market information, paralyzing circumstances or trading opportunities. It is your mind—you run it! The lists below describe the kind of imagery that enhances one's trading performance.

The winning state of mind

- Anxiety-free
- Self-trusting
- Confident
- High self-esteem

Psychological characteristics of the winning state of mind

- Expect the best of yourself.
- Establish a personal standard of excellence.
- Create an internal atmosphere for success based on compelling motivation and focus.
- Communicate effectively with yourself; see yourself as positive, resourceful, self-empowering.

Visual imagery that enhances performance

- Picturing success
- Seeing yourself in control
- Looking competent, relaxed, confident, positive
- Viewing a positive visual image that improves your performance

Auditory imagery that enhances performance

- Hearing the voice of confidence
- Saying to yourself "I knew I was right"
- Listening to the voice of positive expectation

Kinesthetic imagery that enhances trading performance

- Body feels light, confident
- Body is energized, strong
- Focus is direct and alert
- Breathing is relaxed, effortless, long, and deep

FIGURE 2.6   Internal Process for Enhancing State

Visual	Auditory	Kinesthetic
brightness	loudness	even
color	duration	warm
contrast	pitch	cold
distance	tone	pulsating
location	location	intermittent
shapes	direction	strong
size	rhythm	relaxed

Positive beliefs that enhance state

- I believe I am or will be a successful trader.
- I believe I can achieve excellent results in my trading.
- I believe I can identify and execute winning trades.
- I believe I can trade with confidence.
- I believe I can trade effortlessly and automatically.
- I believe each day's performance is fresh.
- I believe I am personally responsible for all my trading results.
- I believe I can be successful without being perfect.
- I believe my performance as a trader does not reflect on my self-worth.
- I believe one bad trade is just that.
- I believe trading is a process.
- I believe that by believing in myself and in any proven methodology and by approaching trading each day with a fresh positive state of mind I possess the ultimate trading edge.

Mental Conditioning

The psychological skills necessary to trade successfully require ongoing conditioning. They must be practiced day in and day out. They are at least as important as your daily chart work!

In an article that was presented at the Dow Jones Telerate Conference, "Gamblers and Risk Takers: What's Luck Got to Do with It?", Joanna Poppink, a psychotherapist who specializes in working with professional traders and investors, writes, "To survive and keep your balance you need to be clear in your decision making and sure in your actions. Every choice you make involves some kind of risk, including the choice to do nothing." More than ever you need to understand the difference between a gamble, which has a high probability of loss, and a calculated risk, which has a much higher probability of a positive outcome. Poppink distinguishes the traits and tendencies of gamblers from calculated risk takers. The following lists contrast the two groups.

The gambler

- Motivation derived from desire for excitement and danger
- Crowd driven
- Highly emotional
- Blames others or luck for bad outcomes
- Lingers over losing choices and wins not taken
- Is influenced by unacknowledged fantasies of what is possible
- Will risk more than can afford to lose
- Acts on impulsive decisions
- Is unaware of unconscious motivation
- Acts out of sense of superiority or "magical thinking"
- Gets high and feels powerful on a win, gets low and feels worthless and small on a loss
- Infuses ego into risk choices
- Lacks discipline and invests on wishful fantasy rather than recognizing reality
- Hides losses and is secretive about taking chances
- Procrastinates (building up excitement levels)
- Follows a favorite method no longer useful or relevant
- When losing will take increasingly bigger risks to catch up
- Looks for the one big win or score that will result in bliss

Poppink observes that one's level of anxiety to "jump in" or fear of pulling the trigger on a trade is normal, as is any step into the unknown. However, the magnitude, duration, and degree of anxiety is a good indication of whether the individual is engaged in a gamble or a calculated risk.

The calculated risk taker

- Contains and manages emotion
- Is aware of irrational factors swaying a crowd
- Takes responsibility for results
- Does not waste time with what might have been
- Acknowledges personal fantasies and resolves or disregards them
- Risks a tiny fraction of equity on any individual choice
- Concentrates on a realistic long-term strategy
- Knows personal abilities and limitations
- Is hardworking and open to new ideas
- Stays emotionally even during wins and losses
- Easily resists risks that do not fit within defined risk limitations
- Is open about risk taking
- Proceeds in a serious, conscious manner
- Stays alert to present trends
- Follows predetermined guidelines of safety
- Analyzes situation, observes own reactions, and makes realistic plans

Poppink concludes her composite of gamblers and risk takers with this observation:

> To be a reasonable risk taker requires that you address each tendency within you that propels you to gamble. At best you resolve it. Minimally you contain it. Sometimes you can do it on your own, some issues require help to address and resolve.

Once you can manage your emotion and follow your own reasonable guidelines you can take calculated risks. And through calculated risk taking, you're sure to increase the good luck in your life.

The Essential Psychological Barriers to Calculated Risk Taking

The following list represents the market behaviors that prevent most traders from achieving the results they desire in the marketplace.

- Not defining a loss
- Getting locked into a belief or magical thinking
- Losing control of a trade or opportunity
- Emotional trading or investing
- Hesitating or procrastinating about a market opportunity
- Loss of focus
- Being more invested in being right than in having a successful outcome
- Not consistently applying your trading system
- Not having a well-defined money management system
- Not being in the right state of mind

The following discussion describes in detail each psychological barrier and advises specific ways to correct these inhibiting behaviors in order to optimize calculated risk taking.

Not Defining a Loss

It is essential for the trader to have clearly defined stop loss points based on his system or methodology. The reason for this is that in the rough-and-tumble of market action the trader needs to be able to react automatically to an unexpected market condition. No one enters a trade assuming it will result in a loss. No one buys expecting that the market has topped out; conversely, no one sells expecting the market to rally to new highs. However, this occurs all too often. So upon entering any market, it is important that you have defined your downside before, not after, you enter a trade. If you are afraid to take a loss, don't trade.

Getting Locked Into a Belief or Magical Thinking

That is exactly what it is—prison. As George Segal succinctly put it, "The market is the boss." Your belief that silver is going to the moon or the dollar is going to hell in a handbasket is irrelevant. The market tells you everything! Listen! Remember what Yogi Berra said: "You can observe a lot by just watching."

Losing Control of a Trade or Opportunity

There is an old Henny Youngman joke that was popular in the early 1960s at the time the Boston Strangler was not yet in police custody. A man is sitting in his living room, reading the evening newspaper, when he hears a knock at the front door. Walking up to the door but not opening it, he asks, "Who is it?"

The psychopath answers, "It's the Boston Strangler."

The man walks back into the apartment, goes into the kitchen, turns to his wife, and says, "It's for you, dear!"

I always relate this anecdote at my seminars as an analogy to taking a trade that you have no control over, from someone else. In other words, a tip is like getting Boston Strangled. Don't do it! This is one door you don't want to open.

Emotional Trading or Investing

Trading like you're a kamikaze pilot on his 44th mission? Perhaps you're feeling betrayed, angry, like you need revenge. Snap out of it! You're going to crash land.

The opposite of kamikaze trading is euphoric trading. You're feeling absolutely invincible. Heroic. Untouchable. Look out!

Hesitating or Procrastinating about a Market Opportunity

You've done all the work—daily, weekly, and monthly charts. You've studied Gann, Fibonacci, Wycoff, and Elliott Wave. The market comes right down to your number, line, and area, but you can't buy it!

Loss of Focus

There are so many distractions in the market. How do you keep your focus clear, laser-straight? How do you get beyond all the head fakes?

Being More Invested in Being Right Than in Having a Successful Outcome

In almost every trading room throughout the world, there are people who run around announcing to their colleagues that they have the high/low of every move in almost every market. What they don't possess are profits. The name of the game is making money. And yes, it's only a game!

Not Consistently Applying Your Trading System

If it's any good, you have to use it consistently. As the saying goes, "If you don't use it, lose it."

Not Having a Well-Defined Money Management System

You have heard this one many times before, "But the trade looked so good, so right." The object of money management is preservation of capital.

Not Being in the Right State of Mind

In my experience, over 80 percent of all trading failure is the result of not being in the right state of mind. The right state of mind produces the right results. As Gene Agatstein observed when I interviewed him in *The Innergame of Trading*, "You get exactly the results you want. You produce your own success."

In the final analysis successful risk taking is calculated, unemotional decision making based on probability theory in the context of a statistically reliable trading system. In operational terms it is overcoming your personal psychological biases for certainty, control, and aversion to loss and adopting a program of calculated risk based on planning, analysis, and discipline.

Critical Factors in Determining Calculated Risk Taking

- Patience
- Discipline
- Strategy

- Expertise
- Motive
- Goals
- Money Management
- State of Mind

FIGURE 2.7   Trader Response

Trader Response	Calculated Risk	Uncalculated Risk
Patience	Wait for opportunities to materialize based on well-thought-out game plan.	Little planning; reacts according to personal whim.
Discipline	Sees the big picture; responds deliberately.	Emotional, anxious; often confused about what to do.
Strategy	Highly planned; limits losses; lets profits run.	Little planning; does not rely on consistent methodology.
Expertise	Well prepared; has done the necessary homework.	Little market knowledge; unprepared.
Motive	Long-term motive, (e.g., intellectual challenge).	To make money; instant gratification.
Goals	Clearly defined.	Ill-defined.
Money Management	Highly controlled risk/reward ratio.	Little or no control over risk/reward ratio.
State of Mind	Positive, resourceful, empowering beliefs and focus; high level of self-esteem and trust; relaxed and confident.	Nervous; anxious; believes the worst will happen. Focus is distracted. Trades in conflict.

3

Technical Analysis
and Risk

*One of the things that I pride myself on
is not having an ego about this business.*

—*Arlene Busch*

It seems to me that a discussion of risk would not be complete without relating it to the marketplace.

Money Management and Risk Management

Although many traders use the terms money management and risk management interchangeably, I prefer to think of these concepts as separate issues. Money management refers to the overall use of capital as it relates to total equity committed to the markets. For example, if you were to commit $100,000 to your program then you would need to decide how you will approach the risk on this total. You may allocate equity to different asset classes and then determine the maximum exposure for each of those elements. Or as many traders do, you may decide on the exposure of your equity on a trade-by-trade basis. Usually, systematic traders will risk from .05 percent to 2 or 3 percent per trade. Discretionary traders very often will expand those parameters, but keep in mind that every successful trader will have a money management concept in place.

Risk management refers to the way traders control the risk on each trade, both on an individual basis and as part of the overall portfolio. Many traders will weigh the volatility of each market or security they are trading and adjust the risk for that particular market. Some will take the standard deviation, or the average range over some time frame, or use full value to determine the risk. These are just some of the methods used; the various methods are endless. For many, the simplest approach to the problem of risk is to calculate exposure for each trade and then superimpose that risk onto the entire portfolio. This will give you individual and portfolio exposure each day. If there is any lesson to be learned here it is that all successful traders have some mechanism in place that allows them or forces them to constantly evaluate risk.

Technical Analysis

Technical analysis is not so much trying to find the profitable trade but a tool to calculate risk and formulate a plan of action on a consistent basis that will maintain the level of risk most desired by the trader. This book is not a book on technical analysis, nor is this chapter meant to be a primer on the subject. However, a discussion on the way traders may use technical analysis is useful and is therefore presented below.

Trends

Trend following and trend identification are the most basic tools used by traders to identify trades. In our previous book, *The Innergame of Trading,* Bob Koppel and I discussed trend identification with the focus on entry and the use of trend signals to enable the trader to facilitate taking the trades that are presented. However, my focus is risk, and we can learn much by relating the very simple concepts of classical chart analysis to how traders view risk. The primary methods of trend identification are:

- Linear trendlines
- Moving averages
- Channel breakouts

Linear trendlines. Simple trendlines are usually drawn from low to low to establish an uptrend, or from high to high to establish a downtrend (see Figures 3.1 and 3.2). Variations on this theme are possible by using closes instead of lows or averaging daily ranges and using those points as references.

Moving averages. The oldest and best-known method of establishing a trend is the moving average (see Figure 3.3). In its simplest form, a moving average is usually obtained by adding up a series of closes and dividing the sum by the number of days used in the series. The result is a smoothing of the series of numbers and an effective method of trend identification. Many variations are possible, such as varying the number of days in the series, using an average of the daily range, using highs and lows, and even changing the value of the most recent days compared to the oldest days. The most obvious use of the moving average is in identifying that a trend is established when the close (or whatever variable you choose) is over the average (or under), thereby signaling direction.

Channel breakouts. The channel breakout method can be used on its own or in conjunction with the other methods (see Figure 3.4). We define a channel as a series of days or weeks that is contained within an area of highs and lows (or average of highs and lows). When a market moves through an area that has been established over a period of time, it then signals a trend.

FIGURE 3.1   Linear Trendlines

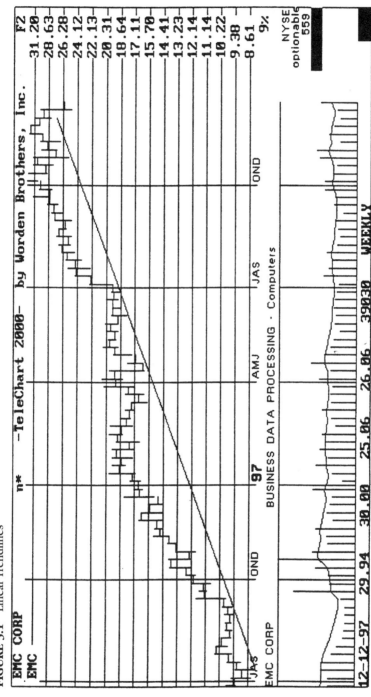

FIGURE 3.2 Linear Trendlines

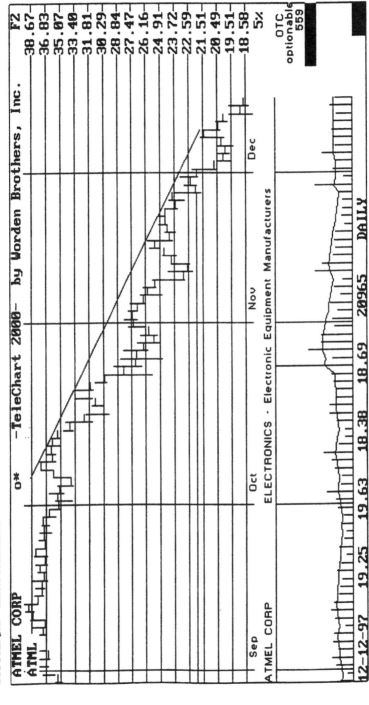

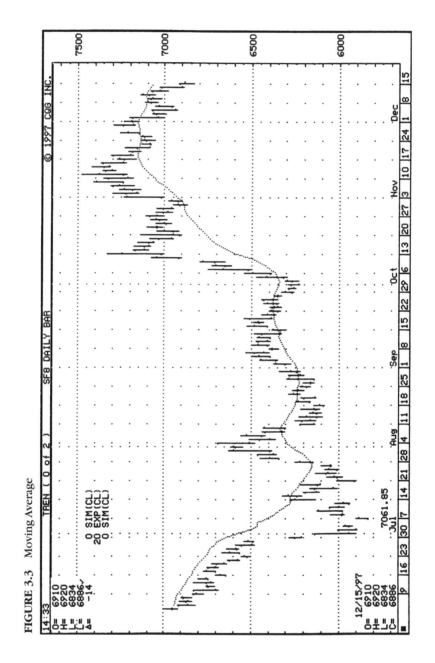

FIGURE 3.3 Moving Average

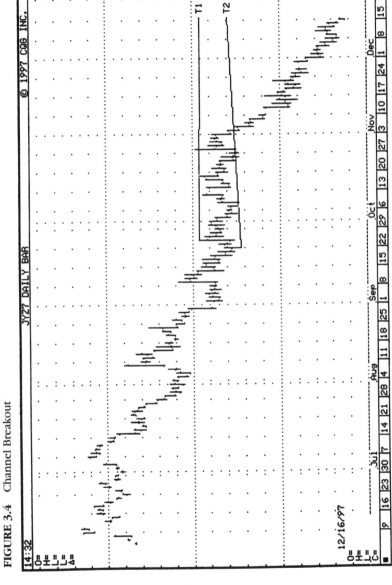

FIGURE 3.4   Channel Breakout

Use as a Risk Tool

The most difficult trade for most traders to make is when the market comes crashing down or rallies sharply to a trendline, moving average, or top or bottom of a channel (see Figures 3.5, 3.6, and 3.7). However, it is precisely at these sometimes climactic moments that risk is the smallest, most neatly defined, and, when taken, the most consistent in results attained. For example, the trader might decide to define the risk as a close under the trendline that was used to make the purchase. Variations on this theme might include using a filter of some percentage close above or below the trendline, or waiting for a low to be established and then buying with that low as the defined risk. There are an infinite variety of combinations, ranging from these simple ideas to sophisticated, computer-driven analogs updated minute by minute.

Moving averages present a greater opportunity for creating complex variations as many traders will use a combination of averages as well as various methods of weighing the time and duration of each average used. For example, a fast-moving average combined with a slower-moving average can define the risk in several ways (see Figure 3.8). Most obviously, if the faster-moving average crosses the slower moving average, it may signal a change in trend. Another approach might be to measure how far the faster-moving average moves above or below the slower-moving average and thereby find an indication of a possible overbought or oversold condition.

The channel may also be used in several ways to manage the risk of a trade. Exiting a trade that was established inside a channel as the market breaks out of that channel is a common approach.

Classical Chart Analysis
and Risk Management

The age of technology has given successful and sophisticated money mangers, some of whom are interviewed in this book, the

FIGURE 3.5 Trendline as a Risk Tool

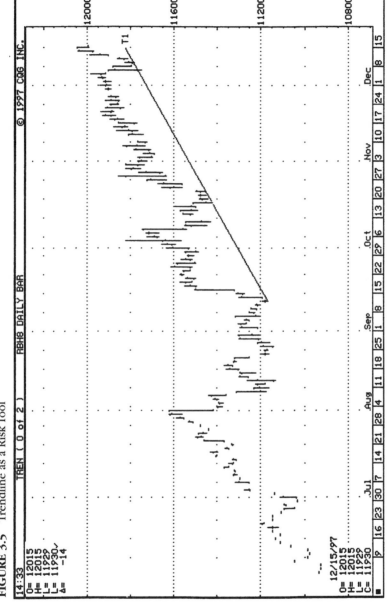

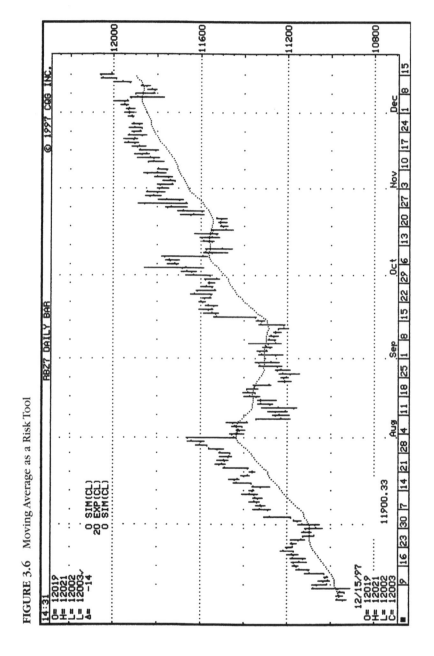

FIGURE 3.6   Moving Average as a Risk Tool

FIGURE 3.7 Channels as a Risk Tool

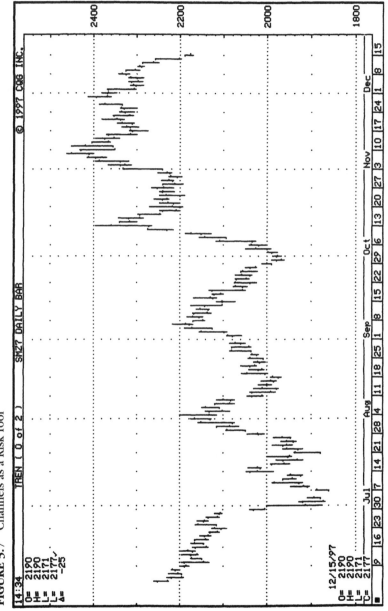

FIGURE 3.8   Multiple Moving Averages

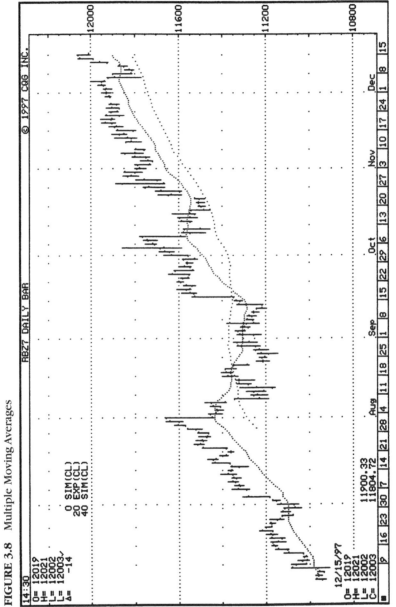

ability to create elaborate risk management systems that tell them not only their current risk profile but also flash exit signals. Many of the essential elements of these computerized systems stem from the simple origins of classical chart analysis or from ideas that flowed from the much-used formulas such as RSI, ADX, MACD, and stochastics.

As we have seen above, identifying a trend in the market, in any time frame by the way, is vital not only for determining market positions but is also a first step in the use of risk management. Even those very short-term, low-volatility systems are capitalizing on the market behavior characteristics that occur repeatedly within larger time frames and are then reduced to repeated behaviors in shorter time frames. It is the reliable nature of the patterns and how the system takes advantage of this reliability that makes many of these systems so successful. Controlling risk in this instance is by the consistent use of high-probability trades over a very short time frame. This concept and some of the patterns referred to are covered in my book *The Day Trader's Advantage.*

Daily or Two-Day Patterns

These include at least five patterns (see Figure 3.9).

1. Outside Day (OD) occurs when the day's range is above and below that of the previous day's range. The day following an outside day can usually be traded by buying dips and selling rallies.
2. Inside Day (ID) occurs when the day's range is below the high and above the low of the previous day's range. Inside days are often followed by increased volatility and should be traded by buying the breakout above the previous day's high and selling a breakout below the previous day's low.

FIGURE 3.9   Two-Day Trades

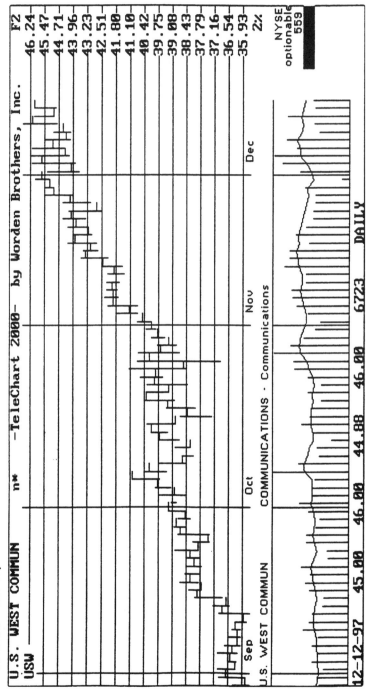

3. Constricted Range Day (CRD) occurs when the range contracts to the smallest range of the past several days. Sometimes the market will contract over two or more days. Patience here can provide opportunity. This is another pattern where the trader should be prepared to trade the breakouts in either direction.

4. Wide Range Day (WRD) is a range that is considerably larger than the past several days. Wide range days are usually followed by trading range days, and the trader should look to buy breaks and sell rallies.

5. Two-Day Highs and Lows occur when markets tend to test the previous day's high or low and can provide the lowest risk trades available. When the trader can combine these tests with either a computer number setup or a chart setup, it becomes a very low-risk, potentially high-reward trade.

Retracements

Once trends are established the problem one faces is low-risk entry. Retracements in a trend give the trader the opportunity to enter a market and define and manage risk (see Figure 3.10). As we stated in *The Innergame of Trading,*

Markets tend to retrace a third, a half, or two-thirds of the previous move. Many traders get caught up in exact numbers (e.g., .384, 618, etc.) and forget that a few ticks is not meaningful in a dynamic and fluid marketplace. If a market retraces 50 percent of a previous move and shows signs of finding support then the trader has a lot of information with which to make a high-percentage, low-risk trade.

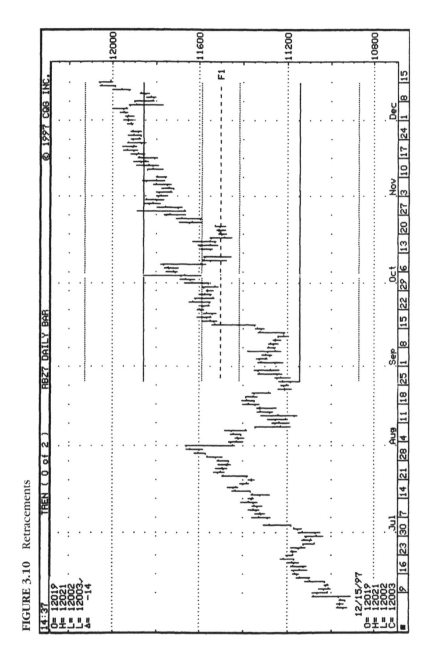

FIGURE 3.10   Retracements

Continuation Patterns

After retracements, continuation patterns that develop repeatedly during an established trend are some of the most reliable, low-risk patterns to use to enter a market. These patterns usually are mere pauses in the trend. Their names describe their shapes: triangles, flags, and rectangles (see Figure 3.11). Traders can control risk by developing systematic approaches for using these patterns at the place of lowest risk and highest probability for each. For example, buying the reaction to the low end of the triangle offers an opportunity to enter with the trend, or, as some traders like to do, buy on the breakout over the trendline drawn from one triangle high to the next triangle high, or a new high for this move.

The point to remember is that these are patterns that may be used to quantify and therefore manage the risk of each trade. In fact, any of the preceding ideas and patterns have the potential to be incorporated into a trading method with the sole purpose of acknowledging and controlling risk. The essential point is that technical analysis provides an operational method for the trader to understand and calculate risk effectively.

Let's turn now to the top traders and see how they manage and control risk in their market operations.

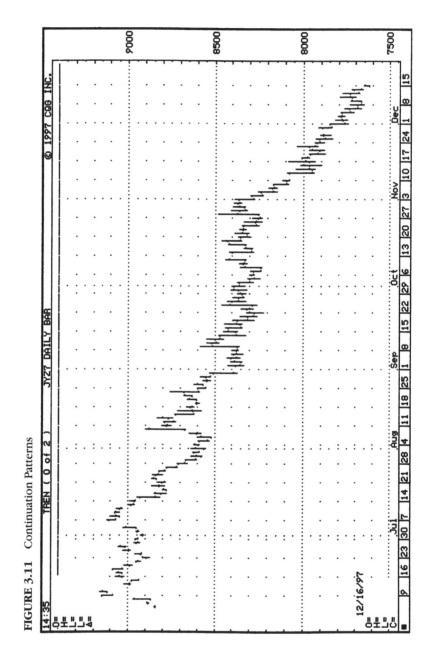

FIGURE 3.11   Continuation Patterns

4

Jeffrey Silverman

Jeffrey Silverman is a member and director of the Chicago Mercantile Exchange. He is an independent trader specializing in agricultural markets.

Q: Jeff, what first attracted you to speculating?

JEFF: To become rich beyond my dreams! I remember discussing this very point with my finance professor at MIT. He pointed out that where there is leverage there's a chance to make a lot of money, but there's also the risk of losing a lot of money.

Q: So the prospect of getting rich was the overriding factor?

JEFF: Yes.

Q: Is that still true today?

JEFF: Well, frankly, speculating, that is trading, is a game. And making money is the object of the game. Dollar signs are just the way you keep score. I remember reading somewhere in an investment book that to trade and to continue to trade successfully you've got to take a meaningful stake in the market; the size of the position you trade and the amount of risk that you carry must be enough to keep your attention. If it doesn't get your adrenaline pumping, you aren't going to pay attention to it, and you're going to let your money slip away because of a lack of interest. So in other words the position has to be meaningful. Which means there's always a tension between maintaining discipline and not overtrading; trading large enough, considering your capital, in order to stay in the game. Again, because if it doesn't hold your attention, you won't play the position well. This is assuming risk is always measured against the background of your individual psychological ability to withstand the risk in the game.

It's kind of hard to quantify this, but to my thinking, in very personal terms, I have a certain amount of money that is dedicated for trading and that sum will keep me in the game. I've got money put away for my retirement, which isn't that far away. The most important thing is I'm actually doing what I love to do, so why would I choose to retire? For me, speculating, calculated risk taking, ironically is almost like a psychological requirement, an addiction if you will! To pursue this metaphorically, I carry around the needle in the form of a portable hand-held quote machine that will give me relevant market information in any major city in North America. I always have a position and an opinion on pretty much every option of all the markets that I trade.

Q: To stay with your analogy, you have to feel the prick of the needle. Is that right?

JEFF: Yes, you've got to get a little rush or the game isn't going to be any fun. I'm reminded of a story that I heard involving two of my professors back at MIT. One was Paul Samuelson, the

Nobel laureate and author of economic textbooks, and Paul Cootner, the famed "random walk" theoretician who studied the financial markets. This goes way back to the late 1960s or early 1970s. At the time Samuelson was long the soybean market. He was making a lot of money, over $100,000, and everyone, including Cootner, knew it. So as the story goes, Samuelson asked Cootner what he thought of the soybeans, and Cootner said, "I think you've made a big enough profit. Take the money!" To which Samuelson retorted, as only an economics professor would, "Paul, I didn't ask you about my utility function; I asked you what you thought about soybeans!"

I think this anecdote illustrates an important point about speculation: In the final analysis risk taking is all about individual utility function. For me this means that in order to get involved in a market, I've got to be willing to make a substantial bet; there's got to be a significant profit potential in order to get me interested. And of course, there's got to be some substantial risk, because I know from past experience that the profit isn't there unless there is risk attached. When I put a position on, I automatically assume that the first thing that's going to happen is that the trade is going to go against me, often for a fair amount. Given the size that I trade, I can never expect to catch the exact bottom or top. So I anticipate and in fact expect loss, and I guess for me that lowers the anxiety because I anticipate the stress of the risk. In fact, I would go so far to say that it is my whole attitude toward risk that allows me to trade on a large scale and lets me make the kind of money that I do, because in essence it all comes down to my ability to withstand the risk.

Q: What do you think are some of the psychological biases that people have relevant to risk that prevent them from being successful?

JEFF: I think to be successful, you've got to figure out how to make the transition from being a small trader to being a large one. And this boils down to something that I heard Joel Greenberg say. As you know, Joel is the current vice chairman of the Chicago Mercantile Exchange. He said one should trade the commodity positions like they're stocks and put up roughly a third of margin requirements; in other words, way undertrade your money. The way I made sense of that remark was to think about trading the market, whatever the size of your trade, as if you're a thousand-lot trader. If you trade like a ten-lot trader, you have the luxury of being able to change your mind a dozen times over the course of a day or a week or a month; you don't learn how to develop the patience of putting on a position where you really have to stick your hand in the fire to catch the big moves. You see, if you're never psychologically able to catch the big moves, you'll be constantly chipping away, and the cost of execution—getting in and getting out—will kill you and eventually eat up your profits over time. The only way that I know how to make money is as a position trader, and that's really what I've always done. It is of course true that I own a membership to get my costs of trading down to the lowest possible level, but the key to my success still is to come up with a long-range idea and sit with a position for the duration of the move. And so whatever size I'm trading, I still trade it as if it is a huge size, as if I'm the thousand-lot trader of whom I was speaking.

Q: Jeff, what do you think the thousand-lot trader specifically does differently from the smaller trader? Obviously you've cited the example of the smaller speculator moving in and out. But in an analytical sense, do you think the larger trader is doing something different?

JEFF: Yes. He's buying in front of the bad news. He's buying when you have to be absolutely crazy to buy! You know, Warren Buffett refers to the market as a manic-depressive business partner, and every day he puts a price on the business. Some days the partner is manic, some days he's depressive, and it's your job to consistently put a price on the business; you have the option of buying or selling the business to him at that price. And it's your job when he's totally manic to say,"You know what? You can take this business and shove it! Thank you very much, it was a nice ride!" And when he's totally depressive, putting a low price on everything, you need to have the ability and the courage of your convictions to stand up to the risk and buy. Of course, everybody will think you're crazy for buying when it's depressive, but that's when you get rewarded. You get rewarded in this business for taking risks, for putting your hand in the fire, for doing things that other people are afraid to do.

You have to be willing to accept risk. You've got to buy it when there's nothing but despair around you. And in fact, your own internal feelings of despair about the long side of the market can be a very good indicator that it's the right time to be buying. I often laugh about it when the cattle market gets really good and the meat packers go out and buy cattle like crazy. I say to myself, they're revving up the motorcycles and jumping over the fences to buy cattle. The cowboys are breaking out the cases of Dom Perignon, and they're not even opening the corks; they're just breaking the bottles on the back of the pickup. And you know, that's the time everyone is saying it's better than "Miller time." That's the exact moment when you've got to sell out your entire position. And invariably, Mr. Market is highly manic at that moment!

Q: How do you prevent buying your own manic feelings and selling your own depression?

JEFF: That's what discipline is all about. When you're feeling manic, you've got to develop the discipline to recognize the internal signs and take the money. And when you're feeling depressed, you've got to avoid jumping out the basement window and buy the market.

Q: And your assessment of risk at those points, whether you're feeling manic or depressed, is just a purely subjective response that you've learned to monitor within yourself to trade effectively, is that what you're saying?

JEFF: Yes. When you come to a situation where you're saying to yourself, God, you have to be crazy to buy the market here, that's very often within a fraction of the time you should be buying it. And if you aren't willing to accept the risk of buying it and having it go against you, you can never get a chance to buy it close to that level again. After the market has turned, rarely are you able to buy it at that level; you're constantly reevaluating and you don't catch the big move. You may catch a little piece or several little pieces of a bigger move, but it's different. Too often you're too long when everything looks "go," and that's when you should be getting out. That's the trap that the small trader falls into. He never can become a big trader because he's not willing to think like and trade like a thousand-lot trader; the size of his position is, in fact, a handicap, and he has to do things differently because of it.

Q: What you're saying is contrary to certain common sense or conventional understandings of the market: that trading a very large position or trading like a large trader gives you a degree of intellectual and psychological distance to judge risk.

JEFF: That's the way I perceive it. It's purely based on my own personal view of risk versus reward—utility function, if you will.

Q: The conventional wisdom on Wall Street is not to be a bottom picker and cautions against attempts "to catch a falling dagger," but what you're saying is, be prepared to catch it at the right moment, is that correct?

JEFF: Yes. I mean, if you go back and look at the examples that Warren Buffett has written about, for example, when he bought American Express in the midst of the salad oil scandal, it proves that you must be there at the point of perceived greatest risk.

Peter Lynch talks about "worsification" as opposed to "diversification." The point is when they "worsify," that's the time to buy!

Take a look at the cattle market. It's now October 10, and we're getting a tremendous amount of negative news entering the market: a continuous information flow about how e-coli bacteria is destroying the U.S. meat supply.

Q: But McDonald's is still selling hamburgers! My kid is still ordering cheeseburgers and french fries!

JEFF: The industry has got a lot of cattle on feed, particularly compared to a year ago when they were restrained from having any cattle on feed because they had $5 corn. They are putting up $700 or $800 a head and they're very optimistic. These guys are the ultimate large traders because when they roll the dice, they make or lose $100 a head, and they do it on 100,000 head of cattle. And they're probably in the process of losing money for the next three or four months. They've gotten overexuberant this past spring and summer, and they've filled up the feed lots. What we're seeing is the result of their overexuberance this past summer; the natural consequence is today's low prices. But as you look out over the next two years, there's smaller numbers of cattle on farms and ranches. Sooner or later the feeder cattle supply is going to be tightening substantially, and feeder cattle are going to be going significantly higher. When does this all happen? I don't know. But I do know at some price, perhaps at $63, as in this past summer when you killed 720,000 cattle a week, the market will stabilize. But right now everybody's very bearish when there's only minimal downside risk.

Howard, I would also like to add this. I think if you're a professional dealer like myself, who's constantly studying the fundamental and technical aspects of a few closely related markets, you can stand in the way of freight trains. But if you're a hedge fund manager or CTA, the approach and thinking are different: you want to diversify the portfolio over a lot of different markets, and you need a time-tested computerized system that enables you to trade them. In that case you're trend following, and that's what you do. The overall portfolio just grinds forward, day by day; every once in awhile there's a hiccup, but basically it treks forward, and it's without discretion. It's the difference between running an organization as opposed to being an iconoclast who's willing to go against the crowd. In exchange politics I very clearly see the difference. There is the local trader who's got his own opinion about everything, who's willing to stand up to convention, and the guys who choose a career as a broker, executing orders for customers or running a clearing operation; they're involved in organizing, meetings, and it's a whole different attitude. They have a desire to control and minimize risk and to develop a business almost as if it were a chemical plant. For them it's all about calculated and organized process. Whereas traders stand there and watch coins flip, portfolio managers design clocks that are going to work, and they get their joy out of doing that. Local traders are there to pounce on situations and make their killing in the market and then get the hell out of there.

The point I'm trying to make is that the individual's personality determines where they're going to fit on this continuum and whether or not they are suited for the job of being a speculator or a highly systematized risk manager.

Q: Jeff, as you evaluate your whole career as a trader, and it's been a long and successful one . . .

JEFF: Not without its ups and downs.

Q: You need the downs to have the ups, to use your earlier example. You need to experience depression to understand the euphoria.

JEFF: Yes. I think what is really key is you have to be willing not to care about what other people think of you. You know, you're out there, and you buy the market in size and everybody knows you bought it, and then you take a loss. Generally speaking, your actions are observed in a fish bowl.

I think you need an utter disregard for what other people think. If you're always worried that other people will think you're stupid because you bought something and it went down or you sold something and it went up, you're dead meat. You need a complete disregard of what other people think of whatever you're doing in the marketplace.

Another way of saying this is that you must be willing to take on the emotional risk.

Q: Emotional risk and social risk can be just as difficult to deal with as monetary risk. Which was most difficult for you to overcome?

JEFF: I think it was all of the above. You know, to be a successful risk taker involves a great deal of philosophical and psychological understanding about the market and yourself. In truth, I've made an extensive study of the market and myself! It's very difficult. You've got to have a big ego to take on the market and say I'm right and the world is wrong. And part of that whole process . . .

Q: I think it's confidence more than ego. I mean, you need a lot of ego, but you also need the strength of conviction to be able to think that your opinion is good enough to be right.

JEFF: . . . and the rest of the world's opinion is wrong. Because that's really what you're saying.

Q: Exactly.

JEFF: Remember, the price that people agree to in the pit is not the price that people think is going to exist in the future. It's the price that both sides vehemently agree won't be there.

To get back to your original question, for me, worrying about what other people thought was tied up with my own ego and influenced whether or not I could admit I was wrong. As I said before, you have to be able not to give a shit about what other people think. Once I didn't care any longer about that, I was able to trade more like the thousand-lot trader than a small speculator.

I really don't remember exactly when that happened. But I do remember suddenly realizing that what I was doing, worrying about what other people thought, was inefficient and worked against a successful risk-taking result.

Q: Was there a particular incident or trade?

JEFF: I don't remember any specific incident. There is a funny thing that happened to me earlier this year when I had been crusading the short side of the hog market in the face of all the bullishness that was pervasive in the wake of the foot and mouth disease killing the Taiwan herds. I was taking a lot of heat in the market because I was short and the market was rallying sharply. Traders were giving me a lot of personal jabs. I heard some stories on the floor that traders were saying "We're going to get Silverman this time." I heard a veteran trader in the pit replied, "Yeah, you've really pushed Jeff to the wall; he's down to his last $10 million!" I thought that was really hilarious. Ultimately, I have my opinion and they have theirs. When the market was going against me, I was saying to myself, those guys are going to need me later to let them out of their long positions.

Q: You were saying this to yourself?

JEFF: Yes. I also said it to them. I believe I've gotten it down to where I don't have any ego. I'm trading the market, not my money, not what the market thinks of me. I buy it based on what I think the market's going to do: go up or down. I don't care where it's been. I care about where it's going. I never use a rearview mirror. I look forward to what I see happening in the future. I do all the things that a successful trader needs to do, which I've learned pragmatically through making a lot of mistakes and watching other people make mistakes. Also by watching the really good traders do things and figuring out what they do. It's all part of my ongoing education.

Q: What is the most important thing you've learned that helped your trading?

JEFF: The concept we've discussed—that whatever size you're trading multiply it by a factor of ten and force yourself to think about timing your entry into the market as if you were trading a position that was ten times the actual size you're willing to trade.

Recently I was reading a book about maintaining mental balance in the face of stress. It talked about the difference between "stressors" and "stress." "Stress" is the measure of the combined impact of a bunch of "stressors"; depending on whether you anticipate the stressor, it may or may not have a significant impact on you. Certainly losing money on a position is a stressor. What I've done, I believe successfully, is learned how to eliminate the pressure from stress because I anticipate the loss. You know, I put on a position, I anticipate that the news is going to get worse, and I'm mentally prepared for the risk.

Q: I hope you don't get disappointed when it goes your way!

JEFF: It's rare. In fact, it's so rare that I don't think we have to consider that as a possibility from my perspective, Howard. I get paid for taking risks. I get paid for carrying positions, and I get paid for pain. If it were easy, widows and orphans would be doing it, and there wouldn't be money for speculators like myself.

I think to a large degree, developing the flexibility to buy something when it's generally perceived as a crazy move was a kind of revelation to me. When everybody is leaning one way in the boat, you've got to look really hard to find a reason to go the other way, and if you can find any kind of a reason, you must be prepared to step up to the plate. You can't be afraid just because going the other way involves risk. That's what you get paid for. When everybody's selling and Mr. Market is totally depressed, you get paid for shouting out loudly, "Buy it!"

Q: How do you know when you're not taking enough risk or when you're taking on too much risk?

JEFF: Well, it's easy to know when you're taking on too much risk. You wake up in the middle of the night worrying.

Q: So, it's an internal sign.

JEFF: The skin on my back breaks out in these huge bumps. When I'm not taking enough risk is when I don't do the every-day disciplined homework that I always do, because it's not oc-cupying enough of my attention. So there's always this tension between having enough risk that the trade is going to force you to pay attention and not so much risk that it's the only thing you have in your life.

Q: As a general percentage of trading equity, how much will you risk on any given trade? Or is it more of an intuitive thing?

JEFF: I think in general terms I don't like to keep more than one-fifth or one-sixth of my money involved in trading.

Q: So you trade between 15 to 20 percent of margin, is that what you're saying?

JEFF: Yes.

Q: And that's how you look at it. You look at it more as mar-gin as opposed to a percentage of trading equity.

JEFF: Right. The exchange's margin calculation is that the daily margin requirements in your account should cover roughly 95 percent of the one-day price movement in the last 90 days. So that if I'm looking at four or five days' worth of extraordinary movement, that gives me some kind of a cushion that's mathe-matically determined more or less by the exchange's risk man-agement program. Once again, I'm mostly dealing with agricultural commodities, not the stock market. But remember, the kind of risk that we saw in 1987, when we had the melt-down, has nothing to do with what's happened the last 90 days! At current price levels for livestock contracts, there's not the kind of potential dramatic fluctuations that you have with the stock market. If I were trading something that had that kind of potentiality I'd have to use a whole different internal criteria. I know this isn't conventional thinking. It gets back to something that my finance professor at MIT told me: governments and individuals can put stocks and currencies in vaults and not look at them for years. But those things can really get away from value. Whereas a perishable commodity that every year has to fall in balance with supply and demand ends up staying relatively close to value. So, in my opinion, pure economics over time can win. Someone who studies economics like myself has a good chance of success.

Q: Jeff, the idea of risk is associated with the issue of uncertainty. Of course, uncertainty is something that psychologically we have to deal with in everything we do. How do you deal with the constant uncertainty of your day-to-day existence in the market?

JEFF: There are people on the trading floor that have their niche of knowing more about what's going to happen in the next 24 hours than anybody else in the world. They can tell you perfectly what the livestock slaughter is going to be, what the cash markets are going to be, what the packers are going to do, everything! And I don't know that having all that "inside" information gives them any advantage over the futures market. Because the futures market is determined by whether people want to buy or sell. I look at the quotes in the futures market as being almost randomly generated. I don't know what the market's going to do today or tomorrow or next week, but I can tell you with what I think is a great deal of confidence what will occur in the next six months or nine months. I'm much more comfortable with that. So I view the short run as noise. I don't know the daily path, where we get from here to there. I know it's going to be with a lot of oscillation and jostling and random walk. It'll be like drunks walking around looking for their keys under lampposts at night. They're looking under the lampposts because that's where the lights are. They can't find their keys because they're not there; the keys are lost away in the dark.

From this perspective, when you get in a situation where the news is all bad, you've got to think about buying it and vice versa, depending of course on your long-term appraisal of the market.

Q: When the daily market action, the noise as you call it, is down more than the average over the last ten-day range, do you go home and say to yourself, I must reevaluate the overall analysis?

JEFF: I'm always trying to reevaluate. The critical question is where you are in terms of risk. The key in terms of risk is not to have so much on that you can't mentally manage your position. You must eliminate bias from the analysis; it's really hard to do an economic evaluation if you've got a position on, which colors your judgment. So I'm always trying to do that. I like to do that at least once a week. When I refuse to do it, I know something's not right.

Q: You already have the answer. It's a symptom.

JEFF: It's a symptom that perhaps I should do something that I'm resisting.

Q: It sounds like the way you deal with uncertainty on a day-to-day basis is basically not to have any. Which is to say when you're stepping into the market you feel there's enough certainty of the market going from point X to point Y, from depression to mania, that the uncertainty is basically nonexistent. Am I correct in saying that?

JEFF: I don't have any uncertainty about where I think the market's ultimately going. I don't allow that cognitive dissonance to get in the way of my actions.

Q: And the daily uncertainty of market movement based on cash prices basically is outside your analysis anyway.

JEFF: I throw up my hands and say, I don't care. I'm short the market, and I walk into the pit, and the guys who are attuned to the daily market (and they live, eat, breathe, drink, and sleep the daily market) come over to me and say, "Is that you selling today? We think it's bottoming here. The market's going to rally. We're going to rally two cents." Well, I'm looking for the market to go down 15 cents, and if it rallies two cents, well, okay, that's the pain that I have to deal with to play this game, to capture the big moves.

I don't know if it's going to rally or not. It probably will. Good luck to them. They can make their two cents. I'm in the game for something different. And you know, I throw up my hands. "Good," I say to myself, "I hope it does rally; I'll sell some more." Part of that also is not having your whole line on. So if you don't have 100 percent of what you can have on, you can absorb the risk that you're willing to take to capture the big move. You can be comfortable allowing for the market to go against you so you can add to your line. But I just don't let the prospect of the market going one way or the other cloud my equanimity on a day-to-day basis. I don't care. It's going where it's going to go, and I want to be on that train, and I don't mind if we don't go from point A to B in a straight line.

We always have to worry about the fact that the news follows the market, not the other way around. Which means that when the market is making its bottom, the news is always the worst. And when the market is rallying, the news is always the best. So when I'm doing my evaluating, I always have to be discounting the news and taking that noise out of the system; I have to remember when the market is rallying what everything looked and felt like when it was on its bottom.

Q: Jeff, do you think other traders can do what you do by approaching the market strictly technically without delving into the fundamentals?

JEFF: Yes. I think if you're looking at it strictly technically you must find something that consistently works for you, oscillators like RSI or volume or open interest that describe the complexion and makeup of the market. In general the technicians won't catch the absolute highs in the market, but they can do pretty well without knowing the fundamentals.

Q: Pat Arbor was quoted in *The Outer Game of Trading* as saying what he did for a living was "take losses." How do you deal with losses?

JEFF: I don't like taking losses!

Q: How do you handle loss?

JEFF: I often try to figure out a strategy where I can be long one commodity and short another that's somehow related, in the most convoluted sense. I do this so that I can withstand the noise and be comfortable that I'm in a position that over time will work out, regardless of the short run. In many ways this seems contrary to what everybody reads in the financial literature: "Keep your losses small and let your profits ride." But you know, in my experience most things that are perceived as conventional wisdom are usually wrong. Some of the most successful traders that I know operate quite well using the opposite philosophy. If you think about a professional fundamentalist's position—if the position was making a lot of money, it would be gone. It's only the position that hasn't worked yet that's sitting on the books. If it was a big winner, for sure I'd take the money. There's a corollary to that, which my partner used to quote: "Nobody takes a profit till you show him a loss." You watch the market go your way and then it has its first correction, and suddenly everybody wants out. Either they're on the first correction or, when it gets back toward where it was, they'll take the money. Of course, you may never get a chance to take the money!

Q: In essence what we're really talking about is how people psychologically view the market, how they're calculating risk and reacting to it.

JEFF: Yes, and I think it is only the large-scale trader, or more accurately, being a trader who thinks large scale, that allows you to buy when it looks like hell. So the noise doesn't get you to do something dumb, like jump out the basement window.

Q: It's like a friend of mine said to me ten years ago; he never owned a piece of real estate that he took a loss on. What he meant by that is when he buys a piece of real estate and the market's good he sells it for a profit. When the market's bad, he holds it until the cycle's over, because he owns it. And all he does is buy and sell real estate for a living. In a way, Jeff, that really describes your operations in the market. I mean, when you go in and take a position you know what your downside is completely, don't you?

JEFF: Yes, I certainly try to.

Q: You try to! I mean, if you're buying, you know; as the thousand-lot trader, you're buying it as if you're someone who owns the real estate, so you know it's not a realized loss until your analytical parameters are violated, your overall conception of the structure of the market is altered.

JEFF: Right. Something's changed from what I thought should have been happening. And I guess the interesting thing about real estate is they don't give you a quote every day at the close!

Q: That may be a good thing.

JEFF: Yes. So on a day-to-day basis you don't know and in fact you don't care because your investment is not geared to a short time frame.

Q: Do you think of risk management and money management as the same thing?

JEFF: You know, I've never really considered whether there was a dichotomy between the two. I think I might view money management as a very mechanical sort of thing and risk management as somewhat more complicated. In my mind I don't get into a position unless the reward justifies the risk. And that's how I discriminate between trades. Money management tells me how much I should be willing to put into the market, and then risk management tells me to some degree where and what is the appropriate use of the speculative capital that I have to employ in the marketplace. All of this so that I get the maximum bang for the buck. I'm not at all interested in just the maximum bang for the margin buck that I'm committing. And I'm constantly evaluating my positions to determine what I should be holding.

Q: Jeff, what is the riskiest thing you ever did in your life?

JEFF: The riskiest?

Q: Yes, physically or emotionally.

JEFF: I think the thing that probably scared me more than anything else was some years ago I spent a month out in Palm Springs and I saw a Porsche Turbo advertised. I bought it in Phoenix and drove it to Palm Springs. There's a stretch where you can look for 50 miles in any direction. I took this Porsche Turbo to the red line, which was I believe 155 miles an hour. The speed was terrifying. You know, the cactuses were whizzing by. The sun was shimmering on the desert sand, and the car felt like it was flying. Truly, I was terrified. I was moving at 155 for what seemed like hours, but I'm sure it was less than a minute.

Q: Did a market position ever give you that feeling?

JEFF: No. I've never allowed a market position to drive me like that.

Q: To 155, right?

JEFF: Not to anything like that.

Q: The reason I came up with that question was that very often in the conventional literature you read about traders who have had "near death" experiences, and it doesn't have to be literal. I mean, it could be they had a life-threatening illness or they went through a huge financial reversal and after being broke or busting out of the exchange came back somehow revitalized. In fact, a few people who Bob Koppel and I interviewed actually said that as a result of that sort of experience, they were able to sort of let go and not care about the money, as you said before. Because they had the experience of surviving the loss of everything. It provided them with the psychological freedom to calculate and manage risk. So I'm wondering if you had any experience like that, and if so, how that affected your trading and your ability to manage risk.

JEFF: Well, I've gone bust a few times. I've had that, and I've come back. And believe me, I don't want to ever have to be broke again. And that's why I manage things a little differently now than I did in the past.

Q: Jeff, what you said earlier about thinking more like the thousand-lot trader and not being concerned about what other people think of you—was this in response to that kind of experience? And if so, could you just tell me a little bit about that experience?

JEFF: I think in the beginning stages as a trader I'd want to always ride the market to its logical extreme. I was trying to catch every dime and capture the last eighth. When I gave that up then I was bullish when the news was bullish and would have to be long. When I gave that up I realized that when the news was really bullish it was a signal that I should be selling. And when I accepted that as my modus operandi, I developed the flexibility to deal with the cognitive dissonance of risk taking that we spoke about earlier. That was kind of an enlightening moment for me— I could take positions that were opposite to what everybody else wanted to do, opposite to conventional wisdom, opposite to the popular delusions of the moment.

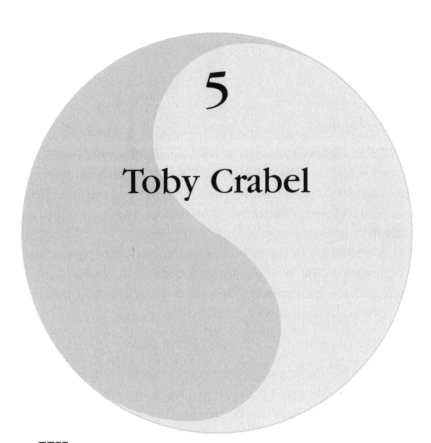

5

Toby Crabel

William H. "Toby" Crabel is the founder and president of Crabel Capital Management, a commodities trading advisor. He has done extensive computer testing of short-term price patterns and is the author of the book *Day Trading with Short-Term Price Patterns and Open Range Breakout.*

Q: What first attracted you to the area of speculation?

TOBY: My dad was interested in trading stocks, and I think it was in 1975 that we went to a brokerage firm. He put me in front of a stock ticker while he was doing something, and I just became fascinated with the whole idea of speculation. Prior to that, my grandmother gave me 30 shares of Eastman Kodak when it was $120 a share. I remember needing the money, and I later sold it for $60. I lost 50 percent and sold the low month of the biggest stock market crash since 1929.

Q: What would you say was your major interest in speculation at that time?

TOBY: I guess I thought it was fun despite my 50 percent drawdown. I thought stocks were fascinating. My grandmother gives me 30 shares of Eastman Kodak, and I'm on the same playing field as Warren Buffett with his shares. That's sort of neat, isn't it?

I don't think I'm any more motivated today than I was when I first started. The excitement that I had for 30 shares of stock then and the excitement I have now for a hundred treasury bonds is really no different.

Q: Do you still attach a feeling of excitement to your trading?

TOBY: It's the challenge. It's not so much excitement right now for me, although it is exciting. It's just an enjoyable activity, a way to live my life. I can be independent and kind of control my own destiny. Trading is also a great business.

Q: How would you say your attitude toward speculation has changed since you made your first trade?

TOBY: It's become more conservative. I have a better understanding of risk than when I sold my Eastman Kodak at a 50 percent loss from peak. I understand more about how to invest. My concept of risk today is much more objective and scientific. When I first started speculating in 1973 or 1974 I was naive and uninformed. I was a beginner.

Q: Essentially, your trading over time has moved away from the discretionary and more toward the mechanical. Is that true?

TOBY: Yes, definitely. I look at risk in a much clearer and more scientific way than I did at the outset. At the outset I knew nothing about risk.

Q: How do you define risk?

TOBY: The main measure of risk that I use is daily standard deviation. I look at the daily standard deviation of the portfolio, which we run at about 35 to 40 basis points. So, I'm looking at the monthly average of daily standard deviation, and include in the analysis peak-to-trough drawdown on a daily and inter-day basis. We look at it every half hour or something like that. Now we have an understanding of where I am relative to the very highest point that I've made on a daily or inter-day basis. Certainly daily close is what we use for practical purposes, but you know, on a very volatile day I'll look at inter-day stuff as well. I also look at how the portfolio is trading, and one of the measures is a move to new highs from the low point. In other words, once I've had a drawdown of a certain amount, I look at how long it takes me to get back to new highs after that drawdown has begun. That tells me something about the continuing health of the portfolio.

Q: Are you assessing the risk of each individual position as you take it on and as it's in your portfolio?

TOBY: We use methods of protecting ourselves in the event of a move against us that are determined by the volatility of the individual markets. So on a daily basis we constantly assess that volatility. And our risk perimeters are adjusted according to that volatility. The important point is that the general perimeters are preset, and we don't have to rethink them on a daily basis.

Q: So your risk management is essentially automated.

TOBY: Yes, exactly. It's completely automated.

Q: Toby, what natural psychological biases do you think people bring to trading that makes it so difficult for them?

TOBY: I think particularly with risk, people don't know how much risk they're taking on. I think a classic example is somebody who trades systematically but the risk side is subjective. In the final analysis that ends up being a subjective strategy. If your allocation methods aren't objective, along with your entry and exit methods, then you have a subjective strategy. And when you're thinking out a trading program or you're thinking about trading, you have to look at it, in my opinion, from not only the system of entry and exit but from the risk management. You have to look at the management of risk within the portfolio. Without doing that, somehow you'll have problems when the markets become extremely volatile, like they have been recently. The tendency for people who don't have every aspect of trading automated is not to trade during unnatural events when the markets are more volatile than usual. So in essence they stop trading. Now I've had this experience personally. When the markets would increase in volatility, I would cut back trading or I'd stop trading altogether. It was a survival mode that I would go into.

Q: Do you think that's the wrong approach?

TOBY: Yes, I do. I think what you have to do is look over a 20-year database and look at all the moves that are possible or could possibly occur when you plan your portfolio. Then determine how much risk is acceptable during these periods so you can participate in these markets.

Q: Toby, in developing your idea about risk, what personal prejudices did you have to wrestle with in order to come up with this successful portfolio?

TOBY: For me, it was a battle between trading for excitement and trading for business—the commitment of making it a business. Over the years, I've continually evolved toward a businesslike approach; right now, and I think at any point if you asked me, I would say I'm more businesslike now than I was last year or the year before. I can tell you, I derive a great deal of satisfaction from seeing consistent returns with relatively low drawdowns. That now is what really is interesting or exciting to me, but it's a different kind of excitement. There's not the immediate high or low that you get from a big move in the market. You can still get that to some extent, but it's sort of incidental. Generally speaking, because of the way I've allocated and the distribution of the portfolio, the chances for any huge wins or losses are a lot smaller. What we're looking at is incremental growth, small gains over a long period of time.

Q: How do you personally deal with this question of uncertainty?

TOBY: I look at what I think the markets are capable of doing to me in a worst case, a price shock, say. And then I say, I need to allocate—what can I live with? What can I allocate to each market on a strategy-by-strategy basis? So what I do is I run that allocation and then I run hypothetical tests on it and look at what my number of contracts would be every day in each market throughout a ten-year period.

Q: So essentially what you're saying is you know that to deal with your uncertainty you have to approach the market in a very objective and scientific way.

TOBY: Absolutely. I think everybody really should do that or has to do that. They have to decide on a level of trading where they can handle the volatility when it becomes the most difficult time to trade. I don't know if that's profound but that's what we have done.

Q: In order to continue to make those trades in volatile markets.

TOBY: Yes, and continue to make the trades.

Q: And how do you deal with the issue of not being in control of the market?

TOBY: Well, the fact is that you are in control of the market at that point.

Q: How so?

TOBY: Because your allocations are at a level that is low enough that you can handle any market. You can emotionally tolerate your system's trading through any type of market environment. If you can do that, then you're in control of your emotions, and that's the only way I know to do it.

The only way to do it is to study beforehand the volatility and allocate accordingly or allocate in line with what you're able to handle on an emotional basis.

Q: Toby, you're talking about a low tolerance as it is. I mean, your approach to the market has a very low tolerance for risk, doesn't it?

TOBY: Yes, relative to the industry, that's true. Our standard deviation is relatively low, so one would call that our risk.

Q: Right.

TOBY: But the other side of it, of course, is that we could have low risk and no returns, that the primary measure is going to be the risk adjustment return, which you're returning relative to your risk. I think that the only way to get a return is to be able to trade through all markets without stopping. And you should never have to stop your trading unless something totally unexpected occurs.

Recently, we had a 3½ percent loss on the day the stock market sold off, and that occurred at one point in the day. I have a portfolio-wide stop or exit point when the portfolio draws down to 4 percent on any given day. So when that happens in one day, I'll exit all positions and start fresh.

Q: You just close out all positions?

TOBY: Close out all positions that we can, and then carry on the next day.

Q: So you actually close out whatever you had on?

TOBY: Yes.

Q: At that point you don't take on any new positions until the next day?

TOBY: We just start from scratch. Now, the reason is because there may be events that I was unable to anticipate. The level at which you come out on your total portfolio has to be a level that should only take place once every 1,000 or 5,000 days. It's going to be something that you just weren't able to plan for because you don't want to come out of a portfolio and not have a chance to make money back afterwards. So, it's got to be a situation where it's very unusual, a worst case.

Q: How do you deal with taking loss?

TOBY: Well, I don't deal very well with taking losses. I've never had to do what I just said, by the way, taking a 4 percent portfolio risk.

Q: But you've come close.

TOBY: Yes, just recently very close. But, you know, we had the biggest stock market break in absolute point terms in history, and in the shortest period of time. And we weathered that with very little drawdown; coming close to those perimeters but never hitting them. This suggests to me that I've done a pretty good job of assessing the risk in what is a worst-case scenario.

Q: So what you have really accomplished is to create a vehicle with which you can survive losses in periods of extreme price shocks.

TOBY: Yes. And each trade has a risk perimeter attached to it already, every single trade in the portfolio. Remember, we've never had a 4 percent loss over a ten-year period. We've never seen a 4 percent loss on the strategies that we use.

Q: The day in question when the market sold off—was it a matter of several positions that you put on going against you, or was it a question of not having specific risk perimeters for a given position?

TOBY: We had a series of positions. We had seven or eight positions that all were wrong in a pretty dramatic way. We were positioned in the market in the wrong direction in almost every market we were in. In order for us to lose that much, you have to have an incredibly large move and be positioned wrong in just about every market.

Q: And that's exactly what happened to you.

TOBY: That's what happened. I've seen that happen maybe three times in the last ten years.

Q: Well, just think about it now. You have a long time before the next event.

TOBY: Let's hope.

Q: Toby, do you think risk management and money management are the same?

TOBY: In my view they are the same thing. They're all part of the same function. It's just a different name for the same thing. You're assessing risk and figuring out ways to handle it.

Q: What do you think is the riskiest thing you ever did or experienced in your life? Have you ever had a near-death experience?

TOBY: The trading certainly has felt bad sometimes when I've had large drawdowns. But I've never really lost the ranch in trading.

Q: Have you ever jumped out of an airplane—with a parachute, of course.

TOBY: You know, I tend not to do things that are self-destructive. I'm a relatively conservative person. So I would have to say no, I'm not a big risk taker.

When I was playing tennis at my best [Toby was a three-time All-American and professional tennis player], when I was tired or a little out of shape or got to feeling overconfident, that's when I would take risks and go for the winner. I would have to do that in order to win. I would have to take added risk. Sometimes when you're playing a better player, that's definitely the case. But in the case of markets, when you're not feeling very strong about things, you're using discretion. Your tendency is going to be to take a few shots that you really shouldn't; you're taking extra risk. Now that's why I believe that this whole thing has to be systematic in every respect, so the risk is completely and unequivocally managed. There are some CTAs and traders that get into events in the market and they close down their trading altogether. They say, "That's it. There's unusual things going on. I can't handle it." They shut down, either when they've made a gain or when they've made a loss. When they have an inordinate upside or they have an unusual drawdown, they shut the doors and say that's it! I used to do that, but now I've decided that that's the worst thing a portfolio manager can do. What you should do is first not have those drawdowns, which means don't allocate too much to any trade or any one market. And secondly, when the markets are really moving, you've got to be there to take advantage of them. And the only way to do that is if you're systematic.

Q: To what extent do you believe your personal understanding of risk contributed to your success?

TOBY: Well, it's unfortunate that I didn't pursue this at a much earlier stage in my career, because I had to learn drawdown through drawdown what it was that I was able to tolerate. In 1981, when I was trading 10 or 15 or 30 percent drawdowns even, it didn't bother me that much. But as I became more and more involved in the business, I began to understand what was tolerable to me and to other people. I made adjustments. So I basically went through this drawdown by drawdown and learned what it was I could tolerate. If you look at my record since then, since the time I started in the futures business in 1980, you'll see a series of draw-downs with my managed programs that became smaller and smaller over the years. So it was a process of self-knowledge or self-understanding that I gained from the experience of losing money.

Q: How has your understanding of risk affected your motivation for trading?

TOBY: Well, my motivation is as good as it's ever been. You know, I still have all the enthusiasm I've ever had about this business, but I direct it in different ways. I don't spend as much energy worrying about the day-to-day risks that I have in any given trade or the portfolio.

Q: So in effect, your approach is your way of dealing with the inevitable anxiety of trading?

TOBY: If you can trade at a level that allows you to sleep at night, you've accomplished that and that's a pretty good measure. If you're losing sleep over your trades, either there's something extraordinary going on in the market or you're trading too large. You have to ask yourself, what's going on? Have I fully calculated the risk of my portfolio?

Q: What advice can you give traders about understanding risk in order to optimize their trading performance?

TOBY: I know that when you start trading you should risk very small amounts of money because you don't know that much about the markets. It would be as if I decided tomorrow to go into the restaurant business, which I know nothing about. The restaurant business is probably just as difficult as any other business, and certainly as difficult as the trading manager business. It would be very stupid of me to take my hard-earned money in the futures business and put it into the restaurant business. My time would be much better served doing something that I know a lot about, unless I just really wanted to run a restaurant. But not knowing anything about the business, I sure would-n't want to put a lot of money into that venture, because the chances of me losing are a lot higher. So, as a starting trader, know that you don't know anything about trading! It's important to treat it as something that you're educating yourself in and to make sure you fully understand risk before you commit too much of your money. In my judgment, the more you learn about risk, the greater is the possibility of your success.

Q: Do you think people can succeed at trading if they don't fully understand how to calculate and evaluate risk?

TOBY: No, I don't think so.

Q: Why not?

TOBY: I think it's just a matter of time before the market puts them in a position to have a catastrophic loss, a loss that will cost them financially and emotionally. They just won't be able to tolerate it. So you must understand risk and develop mechanisms to take care of it. If you don't have that, you won't be able to go on. It's impossible to go on forever without getting caught, unless you just trade so small that it doesn't mean anything. As I said earlier, if you don't know anything about the game, don't bet too much at the outset. Wait until you learn and start to understand what it's all about and what kind of risks you are taking and of course how to manage that risk.

Q: When it comes to understanding risk, what did you learn most about yourself?

TOBY: I've learned that I have different needs in my life. One of them is the need for a very stable, consistent, day-to-day lifestyle; to be risk averse. But also to have an element of excitement in my business.

Q: Toby, the excitement for you is no longer in the trading. The excitement is in containing the drawdown, circumscribing the risk, and having the highest sharp ratio in the industry. Is that right?

TOBY: That is my goal. I'm looking at risk-adjusted returns, not absolute returns. I'm looking for how much I'm able to make with the lowest level of risk. That's exciting to me.

Q: I think what has really come through is that in the beginning the challenge was in the trading and having the return— you know, a great return; in other words, being what used to be considered a great discretionary trader. But now the challenge for you is really in risk-adjusted returns. There are very few guys in the industry, as you know, who can accomplish what you have.

TOBY: In my view, Howard, it's the difference between short-term thinking and long-term thinking. My satisfaction derives from building a steady, consistent business. I'm in the game for the long run.

6

Charles LeBeau

Charles "Chuck" LeBeau is the founder and president of Island View Financial Group, Inc., a firm managing money in the futures market. He is the coauthor of *Computer Analysis of the Futures Market.*

Q: Chuck, what first attracted you to the area of speculation?

CHUCK: Actually, I got started in college. I was a prelaw major at Long Beach State and I happened to take an investment course with Dr. Charles Harlow. You might recognize the name; he was Harlow of Teweles, Harlow and Stone. They wrote several books on investments and taught at Long Beach State.

Q: They wrote about the futures market.

CHUCK: Yes, several books on futures and a couple of books on the stock market. Dr. Harlow was a second-generation commodities trader. He and Teweles and Stone had been given some space in the basement of the Paine Webber office in Long Beach. I used to go down there and help them post charts. They kind of took me under their wing and started teaching me about commodities in addition to the investment course, which dealt primarily with securities. In truth, I just got hooked. That was a long time ago. That was back in 1962 or 1963 when the prices came across the old ticker tapes, which were posted on a blackboard. Of course, there weren't a whole lot of commodities to trade back then, but I found it to be fascinating. I changed my major to finance and decided then and there that I wanted to get involved in the commodities business.

Q: Now what was it specifically about the commodities business that attracted you?

CHUCK: I'm not really sure. Just the idea, I guess, of the potential there, the money that could be made, and the fact that trading was a skill that not everyone had. There were very few commodities traders around at that time, and the whole enterprise just appealed to me.

Q: Was there excitement involved?

CHUCK: Well, somewhat—not as exciting as doing it for real, you know. I was kind of looking over their shoulder and watching them trade, but I thought it was very interesting.

Q: Do you believe that what first interested you in trading still holds the same attraction?

CHUCK: Not so much anymore. The way that I do it now is systematic, and that takes a lot of the excitement out of it. It's much more conservative and therefore less exciting; but I still get up every morning and look forward to going into the office and monitoring what's taking place in the markets.

Q: You say that it's all systematic now. I guess you're talking about being on an automatic trading program, is that correct?

CHUCK: Yes. We've designed a specific systematic approach to trading, and we follow that. It's still very exciting and interesting, I guess, though the emphasis now is more on seeing the outcome of the trades. We're always curious and involved; not perhaps as much as if we're doing discretionary trading.

Q: What natural psychological biases do you think most people bring to trading that makes it so difficult?

CHUCK: I think it's the fear of losses. We're brought up very early to be afraid of doing things wrong. And certainly anything that has to do with our thinking ability or, you know, our logic. Physical activities are somewhat different; we can fail at them because everybody has his limitations and not everybody's a Michael Jordan. But when it comes to intellectual activities, you know, we focus on the score. You get 90 percent or higher right, and you get an A; get less than 65 percent right and you fail. In trading, we fail in an uncomfortable amount. Certainly as a trend follower, the percentage of winning trades is lower than it might be if we're using some other method. But you've got to learn to live with that. And as you know, I'm sure, the secret to successful trading is cutting the losses short, which means there's more likely to be more of the small losses floating around than there are the big winners. So it's the failure rate of the bad trades that I think most people have a hard time dealing with.

Q: Do you have that problem as it concerns the systematic approach that you use?

CHUCK: Oh, I've been doing this for over 30 years now. I guess after the first 10 or 20,000 losing trades, I began to get used to it.

Q: Now you mentioned, Chuck, that you're systematized in your approach, but what personal prejudices do you believe you had to wrestle with in order to effect successful results in your trading? I'm sure going automated must in fact have been your way to cope with any personal biases.

CHUCK: Yes. Actually, having a methodology that's based on some thorough research, in fact, helps you to implement trades as opposed to just trading off of your intuition. Especially if you don't really know if your intuition is all that good. You can lose your self-confidence if you're an intuitive trader after a few losing trades and wonder if you really know what you're doing at all or if you should be in this business! So it's sometimes better in my experience to be operating on a system where you know the probability is that after you make 30 or 40 trades, you can expect profits. You'll know statistically that there's going to be a certain amount of losers along the way, and it doesn't bring in any self-doubt or questions about your individual abilities.

Q: Initially, though, what psychological prejudices did you have to overcome to deal with uncertainty or loss or the lack of control of the market?

CHUCK: Well, I'm not sure. Like I said, I was hooked quite early and maybe I hadn't had enough time and experience. I was very young at the time, still in college, when I started trading and maybe I didn't pick up all those prejudices along the way that somebody more mature and experienced might have. I saw people that were doing it and doing it well and making money, so maybe I had a different outlook than most people who merely read horror stories in the newspaper.

Q: How do you deal with the issue of uncertainty?

CHUCK: Well, that's life. There's uncertainty in all investments, and believe me, I've seen a lot more money lost in the bond market than I've ever seen lost in the futures market. It's the so-called safe investments, when people don't have their guard up, where the big losses tend to occur. People go into the futures markets with their eyes wide open; they know what they're getting into. It's the so-called safe investments that can sneak up and really get you.

Q: How about the idea of not being in control of a market?

CHUCK: Well, I'm not sure anybody's really in control. Who's in control of the stock market or any market, for that matter?

Q: Of course, nobody's in control. The point is, how do you deal with it subjectively? A lot of people can't deal with it and don't deal with it very successfully.

CHUCK: While nobody can control the markets; at best, they need to be able to control themselves. That's the control that we need to look for. Nobody's going to control the markets.

Q: How do you deal with taking a loss?

CHUCK: It's just one more step. Statistically I know that after so many losses we're going to have a profit. It's statistics. Each loss is limited, and the loss puts me one step closer to the next profitable trade. It's putting kind of a positive spin on things, but I think it helps. And it also helps in pulling the trigger on trading to understand that if you do trade and take a loss, it's going to be a small one. And you know—you should know before you trade—what the worst-case scenario is and what the loss might be before you trade. And if you for some reason decide not to do that trade, you'll never know how much the profit might have been, because good traders will let their profits run. So I can sit and say, "Do I put on this trade and maybe take a $900 loss or do I want to skip this trade and maybe forgo a $10,000 profit?" When you start looking at things that way, the trading gets much easier.

Q: How about the idea of coping with a drawdown over a protracted period of time, whether it's several days or, let's say, a couple of months in a row? How do you deal with that?

CHUCK: Well, when you're a trading adviser like we are, you're either making new highs or you're in a drawdown. So we certainly enjoy making new highs whenever that occurs, but that isn't most of the time, unfortunately. We spend much more of our time than people might suspect in a drawdown. And the duration can be a problem. It's a problem for our clients; they don't have the experience and the results of all the testing that we have to give them the confidence to proceed forward. Unfortunately, when we go through a drawdown, it's not so much the magnitude of the drawdown in terms of the dollars lost but the length of time spent in the drawdown. It tends to drive our clients away, particularly when there's a rip-roaring bull market in stocks. They're always thinking about what they could be earning in the stock market.

Q: That's the age-old problem in our business.

CHUCK: Yes. The clients tend to invest near our peaks and tend to withdraw their investments near our valleys. And in spite of what we think is good trading, some clients we'll lose.

Q: Chuck, how do you personally calculate risk?

CHUCK: Well, there's all sorts of risk. It seems like a simple question, but as you know the answer is quite complex.

Q: What are some of your thoughts on the different kinds of market risk?

CHUCK: There's the risk of doing something and the risk of not doing something.

Q: Is the risk of not taking a trade as great to you as the risk of taking one?

CHUCK: It's much greater. That's why we don't skip trades here. We take the trades, and we're willing to accept a small loss if necessary. The big risk, in fact, would be in not getting the potential big profit. There's the risk of the trade! We talked earlier about controlling markets. We can't control the markets, but we can absolutely control our risk, and you know, that's the first thing a successful trader has to address. If you control the risk properly, the profits tend to take care of themselves.

The first thing that we want to do is to always look at the worst case and have protection and a game plan that says if things go wrong, here is what our exposure is and here's what our risk might be. That's normally expressed in a certain amount of dollars on each trade. So before we put the trade on, we have a specific dollar amount. In our case, a number that we very commonly use would be $1,500 on a worst-case scenario on a per-contract basis. However, that doesn't mean that our average loss is $1,500. Hopefully, every trade we make is not a worst-case scenario. We usually have losses that are less than our worst-case scenario, and those loss points are determined on a technical basis with the help of some computer technology. We may initiate a trade and say that the loss on this trade is only going to be $600 if things go according to plan. But there's always an outside chance that things might not go according to plan, and the risk might approach the $1,500 level.

There's a risk that a lot of people don't seem to address properly, and that's the risk of loss of open profits. In the futures markets, as you know, the profits are paid to your account each day, and that's your money. You can actually take it out and spend it and still leave your position on. A person that owns a hundred shares of IBM that has a pay-for-profit can't take that profit and go out and spend it. So very often they get used to thinking, well, it's not really my money yet or I haven't realized the gain. But in futures, you're paid that money, and the brokerage firm will send you a check for it anytime you ask. So those open profits are a potential for loss, and there's this contradiction between the idea of always trying to let your profits run and the realization that when you get back open profits, you're giving back some real money that already belongs to you.

Q: There's a fine line between letting the market do its thing to stay in the trend and giving back open trade profits, isn't there?

CHUCK: Oh yes. That's probably the most difficult thing in trading. Like I said a moment ago, I think the losses you can generally manage pretty well. You can plan ahead for those, and you can put in your stops, and there's a very tight pattern—at least for a good trader there should be a tight pattern of what happens with your losses. But on the gain side, you just never know how big the gain might be. You know, there's a lot of stress, at least for me, in handling winning trades. It always seemed that the winning trades were more stressful than the losers. The losers I always knew and had a plan for. I knew almost exactly what was going to happen on the losing trades. But with the winners you start out and you get $1,000 and you get $2,000 and then it's $4,000 and then $10,000, and you say to yourself, where is it going to end? You just don't know. If you take a $10,000 profit and it winds up being $20,000, you've missed a real opportunity. So it's extremely difficult. The management of good trades is something I don't think enough attention is given to in the industry. It's a real art and a science as well. I think most people should spend less time trying to figure out how to get into trades and a lot more time figuring out how to manage them once on.

Q: How do you deal with getting out of trades?

CHUCK: After years and years of thought and continuous research, which continues as we speak, the best solution so far has been to give a new trade plenty of room. You can't take a small profit and still have a big one. You need to give a new trade some room, not get real enthused about the small profits, and let the trade grow. Once it reaches a point where the profit is extraordinary or well beyond the average, then you need to change that strategy and make sure you're protecting most of it. So a two-stage solution is the best that we've found: You have one set of stops that are used for a new trade, in the hopes that it becomes a big winner. And then there's another set of exits that you implement once the trade is a big winner, so that you don't give much of it back. We try to install a valve in a big trade that allows it to get even bigger, but it doesn't allow a big trade to wind up being a small trade.

Q: Is risk management and money management the same?

CHUCK: Well, they're all tied together in my mind. We're trying to make sure that we progress forward and don't have too many setbacks. And there's always going to be some losses, and there's always going to be some drawdowns. And we want to keep them small so that we can make them back quickly and easily.

Q: What do you think is the riskiest thing you ever did or experienced in your own life?

CHUCK: Well, I was almost killed at the Paris air show in 1965 by an airplane that crashed a few yards behind me and went over my head. You know, I had no control over that. A very scary experience.

Q: Has that experience in any way influenced your market behavior?

CHUCK: I don't really see any connection between the two. We're just talking about risking money, and it shouldn't be anybody's life savings or anything like that. We're taking a limited amount of risk with a limited amount of funds and overall it seems quite conservative.

Q: To what extent do you believe that your personal understanding of risk contributed to your success as a trader?

CHUCK: Oh, I think it's extremely important and I would not have survived without it.

Q: Has it affected your motivation for trading?

CHUCK: Well, I don't know. I see trading as a challenge, and I enjoy doing it, and I feel that I do it well. I think we all enjoy doing things that we think we're good at. I was fortunate in a couple of respects regarding risk to be taught at the beginning by some people that were very good at managing risk. And then later on, when I became a broker, I was able to observe the risks that my clients were taking. I didn't control the trading at that point. You know, I could give advice when it was asked for, but I saw clients trade. Some of them did well, some of them did very poorly. I could see firsthand what they were doing about risk. And by observing the difference between the winners and losers, I was able to kind of see a pattern and develop a strategy and give better advice over time.

Q: How would you characterize the difference between winners and losers?

CHUCK: I think that the key element is not trying to make too much money too fast. There's a tendency to take a small amount of money and think that you can immediately run it up into a big amount of money. There's a tendency for newcomers in the business to trade positions that are too large and to be too active. They feel that the next big trade is just right around the corner. They're always doing something for fear they'll miss out.

Q: What advice can you give traders about understanding risk in order to optimize their trading performance?

CHUCK: I would advise them to err on the side of keeping the risk too small. Start extremely conservatively and increase the risk with some of your profits. If you're going to be aggressive, don't be aggressive until you've made some money. Become more aggressive only in proportion to your winnings. I used to send clients back money out of their accounts on a somewhat unsolicited basis, just to make sure that after a profit run they didn't get overly aggressive and lose it all. And there was some complaining at the time; they always questioned me about it. And I'd say, "Well, take some of the profit. Go out and buy something tangible with it. You'll appreciate it more, and someday you'll be glad you did." That almost always paid off.

Q: Do you think that one can succeed at trading without fully understanding how to calculate and evaluate risk?

CHUCK: No, I don't think so.

Q: Why not?

CHUCK: People who don't understand risk are just going to lose all of their investment. It's just a matter of time, even if they start out winning. You know, not everybody starts out with losing trades. Most losers start out with winning trades and feel that they know more than they actually do; they think they don't need to be concerned about risk. They feel somehow immune to the risks of the market because of their particular talent or skills. That's extremely dangerous. It's just going to get them in trouble. You always hear about how many losers there are in the futures and commodity markets. The losers are the people that don't understand and know how to calculate risk.

Q: When it came to understanding risk, what did you learn most about yourself?

CHUCK: That I had some kind of immunity to it or less fear of it than most brokers. People used to think that I had a very stressful job, that I was always worrying and upset, agonizing over things; I really wasn't. I'm generally very calm, with a positive outlook on things. People would not have a clue as to the size of positions I might be holding, and it didn't affect anything else that I did in life.

Q: What do you think are the principles of successful investment or trading?

CHUCK: Well, I'm concerned about people that feel that market timing is not necessary. That seems to be the prevalent thinking in the stock market, that people can just buy and hold. But I think that's sheer ignorance, and it shows that they know nothing about the history of the stock market. There are many, many ten-year periods where individuals would buy and hold and would have had very substantial losses in the stock market. Somehow today it's viewed as being safe. People that get into the futures markets know they can't buy and hold, so they immediately become familiar with market timing. But there's a whole lot of people out there that are invested in the stock and bond market that don't realize that buy and hold is not the best trading strategy.

Q: Chuck, do you think that the first requirement of a good trader is to determine risk?

CHUCK: Yes, in lots of different ways. The risk to their lifestyle, the risk of their time, the risk of their money, the risk of their marriage. There are a lot of risks in addition to just dollars and cents.

Q: Could you elaborate on that?

CHUCK: People change their personalities with losses. I've had unfortunate experiences with clients who completely changed their outlook on life. They just completely regressed into another personality when faced with a large loss. That's a terrible mistake, to let a loss get so large that it's unthinkable to take. You cannot cope with the consequences of taking that loss; therefore, you lock onto it and allow it to continue, and it can just destroy your whole life. I've seen marriages ruined. I've known a trader or two that committed suicide. I've seen bankruptcies and all sorts of financial problems generated. And it all stems from not being able to take the best loss, which is a small loss. Some people experience a losing trade as some kind of a personal failure and a reflection of their unworthiness. Consequently, it affects their life and it shouldn't. A loss isn't anything important; and if you're going to be a trader, you better get used to that right away.

Q: Chuck, why do you think that you've been able to deal with the issue of risk successfully over time?

CHUCK: I basically started out with the attitude that learning is important. I never had much money to lose, so I always had to watch the losses very closely when I first began trading. And then later on, when I became a broker, I was able to learn a great deal from watching other people's market behavior. I must also add if there's any stress to me in this business, it relates to having to watch and take risks with other people's money. I'd be much more comfortable if it were my own money at risk. I'm always thinking about the attitudes of the clients and the effect of any losses that we might have on what the client is experiencing and feeling. I don't have any problem dealing with losses. I'm confident that they'll be made back, but the clients don't have the benefit of experience to truly believe that and appreciate it.

7

Larry Rosenberg

Larry Rosenberg is a long-time member of the Chicago Mercantile Exchange and is a past chairman of its board of directors. He was an active floor trader for many years and continues to trade successfully for his own account on and off the exchange floor. He is president of Lake Shore Asset Management and PMB, a Futures Commission Merchant.

Q: Larry, what first attracted you to the area of speculation?

LARRY: It seems so long ago, it's hard to remember. But I think the same thing that attracts me to it now: the potential for virtually unlimited gain. The idea of working for yourself, and having your efforts handsomely rewarded. Of course, the downside is the loss. But if you have the makeup to live with it, it can be a rewarding lifestyle. Of course the loss can be controlled through discipline, but you do have to be disciplined!

Q: You started off as a floor trader, and now, in addition to running a clearing firm and an asset management firm, you also still trade your own account. Can you just talk a little bit about how your concept of risk has changed from being a market maker on the floor of the exchange to doing the kind of trading that you're currently doing?

LARRY: The 30 years I spent on the trading floor I was a pit trader and completely discretionary; what some might call seat-of-the-pants trading. I would spread, outright position trade, and scalp. It was just market feel, and I guess that's a feel that has built up over my many years of experience. I was always good at taking a loss, and there was no scientific formula to it. If my pants got a little tight, I knew I was in trouble and it was time to hit the road. Sometimes that could be a major move; sometimes it could be one or two ticks. It all depends on what the situation was and the circumstances were. Since I've moved upstairs I don't think that works. First off, I think a lot of times on the floor I was triggered by the audible, by the sound of the market. A down market has a different sound than an up market. When you come upstairs, it's all visual, and I had to adjust to that. First off, you're removed. You're one step away from the physical action so you have to think about the trade less in terms of reaction time. Upstairs, I think you have to have your priorities clearly set when you enter a trade. Now when I establish a trade, I don't always know where I'm going to take my profit, if there is one, but I always know where I'm going to take my loss. The whole process is much more clearly defined now than when I was a floor trader.

Q: But you still do this in a discretionary way. I mean, you're not a black box trader.

LARRY: No, I'm not black box at all. Although I have developed a few mechanical . . .

Q: . . . tools?

LARRY: Tools, exactly. And a lot of intuition. You know, for example, when I'm trading the grains, I'm not going to take a ten-cent risk when I'm looking for a four-cent profit. But there is still a lot of intuition there. I always do know where my loss is, and I take it at that point, no questions asked.

Q: Do you think that the same things that attracted you to trading 30 years ago still do?

LARRY: Well, the business has changed so much. Personally, I would never go back to the trading floor. It has changed so much. It's just a different place than it was. I don't think there is an edge on the floor anymore. Our marketplace is a global market with computers and information traveling at the speed of light. The edge simply is no longer on the floor. I think sometimes just being on the floor, being too close to the action, is a disadvantage. You react emotionally, and these aren't markets to which a person should react emotionally. I think you have to be very collected and have your game plan well laid out. I do my homework the night before. I generate signals on the markets that I'm looking at for the next day, and those are the only trades I take. If something comes up intra-day in another market, I'll note it and take a look at it after the close, but my whole approach is much more defined and calculated.

Q: Do you prefer to trade a wide portfolio of markets or a single market?

LARRY: I trade just about anything. Usually no more than a few positions on any given day. I've got it down now to where if I'm involved in three markets, that's the cutoff for me. I have stretched it to five on certain days, but I usually find I can maintain a nice feel with three. Perhaps as I've gotten older I've become a little more conservative. If I have three positions, I'm fine, and as I said, I kind of cap it at that.

Q: Larry, I want to follow up on this thing about being more conservative, because I've heard this idea from a variety of traders, both portfolio managers and guys like yourself who have been very successful on and off the trading floor. When you speak about being more conservative, do you think as you've gotten older you've become more conservative about embracing risk, or do you think getting older has expanded your ability to embrace risk?

LARRY: I think when I was younger, trading on the floor, I never really gave serious thought to the issue of risk. I could trade for a year and have three losing days. Risk, for me, wasn't a factor; I just traded. And I intuitively would get out and manage the risk. Coming off the floor, being more objective about the process, I think the risks are far greater. And I think you have to be a little more risk averse. I think getting older allows you to have broader parameters. Your stops are wider. So I naturally trade smaller. Because one of the worst things, and I've learned this the hard way, is that trading larger and then placing your stop at the wrong time can ruin a good position. And I find, in truth, that I can make more money with smaller positions. First, my stop will be in the proper location, and second, I'll stay with the position for the long haul. I won't jump out at the first downturn in the market.

Q: So, you've become more conservative in terms of the size of the position and the risk that you take on that position, but not conservative in terms of an overall concept of risk. What I think you've said is that you can maximize a position by taking a smaller position size. Is that correct?

LARRY: You're right. I manage my risk by the size of the position, because markets are going to trade as they trade. They are still going to do their thing, and you're just going to get blown out with too large a position. I have to manage risk more in terms of the size of my position.

Q: What psychological biases do you think traders bring to trading that makes it so difficult for them?

LARRY: Ego. I think people invest their ego too much in this thing. They equate being right to being smart, being wrong to being dumb. They trade to be right. So that's a big thing, people who trade for ego reasons. There are also people who trade just because they like the action. They forget that it's good business policy not to trade in some markets: crazy days like last week when the slippage in the S&P can be thousands of dollars a contract. Truthfully, I don't know why a person would try to day trade off the floor in something like that.

Q: You know, Larry, I placed an order in the S&Ps one day last week and we were eight handles off the screen market in a fast market situation.

LARRY: $4,000 a contract! I mean, it's bizarre. But again there are people who are strictly looking for the action. I trade as a business. It's my income. And I treat it as a business. I don't try to put ego into it. I know that if I have a position, I focus on nothing other than that position. I'm not starting to think about how I'm going to spend the money, on a new car or vacation. When I do, that's the time to get out because then my ego is getting involved.

I try to be very objective. That's why I like it when I put on a position; to know that I've done my homework at night and the stop goes in. Then it's out of my hands. I'm on autopilot, and frankly it allows me to run my business. I don't have to sit there with my face glued to the screen all day. I think that's a mistake people make, also. You become so mesmerized, your vision turns myopic. You focus on just the quotes, and you really lose sight of the big picture. You start reacting to every up and down move in the market. That's not something you want to do.

Q: What are some of the personal prejudices that you had to wrestle with in order to become successful in your trading?

LARRY: I imagine, like all of us, I had ego problems. Sometimes I'd overbid or overoffer. I mean, I had that experience many times. I don't know if I ever told you this story, but once in the corn pit, at a time when I was usually trading 10 or 20 lots, I bid on 50. I'd never had a 50 lot in my life. This was a monster trade for me. And I heard someone say "Sold!" Of course, I didn't want to look around, because I thought they might be talking to me. And there was the traditional tap on my shoulder and one of the great gentlemen in the history of the business, a man by the name of Ed Byers, said, "Sold, son." I was so nervous I had trouble writing the trade on my card. I knew I was in big trouble. The market was immediately a quarter of a point against me. You also have to understand that my trading account at that time was very small. So, my life is now flashing before me, and Ed Byers looked at me and knew I was having trouble breathing, and he said, "Son, never bid or offer what you're not prepared to take. We did nothing." And he tore up the trade. That was it, and believe me I learned a lot from that experience. It was strictly an ego trade. Ed Byers taught me a very a valuable lesson. A moment after he let me out he went on to sell thousands of contracts.

Q: How do you deal with the question of uncertainty?

LARRY: Of course, the market's always uncertain and I know I can never be certain. In fact, when I get my most certain, that's when I feel I shouldn't be in the trade.

Q: You're saying that when you feel absolutely certain about a trade, you take another look at it.

LARRY: Yes. That's when you take your biggest losses.

Q: Could you elaborate?

LARRY: I've been around long enough to know, as you do, Howard, that I'm never sure of anything in these markets. And when I feel my most certain, that's when my trading antennae go up.

Q: So, a feeling of certainty is like a symptom to reevaluate your risk?

LARRY: That's right. And then I think ego is taking over, and that too is a warning.

Q: How do you deal with not being in control of the market?

LARRY: We're really just pawns in this game. If you begin to think you have control of any of these markets, you have a serious problem. You don't have control and you must know that. The markets are going where the markets are going. I don't care if you are the Bank of England. No individual or institution is bigger than the market. The trader's focus has to be on controlling himself. That's much tougher than controlling the market!

Q: In many ways gaining control comes from giving up the need for control, don't you think? I mean, you get control by having your technical buys and sells placed in the market.

LARRY: Right. Having my orders already placed in the market with tight stops serves that function.

Q: Larry, how do you calculate the risk that you take on any given trade?

LARRY: I'm not very scientific. I know a lot of funds use specific mathematical formulations. I'm still of the old school.

Q: You don't have any specific mathematical algorithms for calculating risk?

LARRY: I can't even spell that!

Q: But you know when you're taking a calculated risk. I mean, you must know intuitively. Is that correct?

LARRY: Oh, absolutely.

Q: How do you determine for yourself what is acceptable risk exposure on any trade?

LARRY: Very simply. What I try to do is I look at a market objectively and say, okay, if the trade's here, I want to be long. If the trade's back here, I want to be out. All right, now how much is that? If it's grains I'll say, okay, if it's five cents I can be long X amount. If it's ten cents, I can only be long half of that.

Q: Do you ultimately break it down to dollars and cents or is it just something you feel about that specific market from years of experience?

LARRY: I don't know that I have a real definitive answer to that, but I always try to look at the market objectively and through experience to know if this is a two or two hundred contract trade. I try to look more to the internals of the market than the dollars and cents. Otherwise I'm focusing more on the money than the market.

Q: Do you think that risk management and money management are the same thing?

LARRY: Yes. The way I approach the market I think risk management and money management are the same thing.

Q: Larry, what do you think is the riskiest thing you ever did or experienced in your life?

LARRY: I've had a few harrowing ski experiences, one where I almost lost my arm, but probably the riskiest thing involved an incident that happened to me in a sailing race. We were racing a boat from Tampa to Ft. Lauderdale around the tip of Florida. It was a couple-day race. We were out in the gulfstream and a gale came through with huge winds. We were racing the boat and winds came through at 70 or 75 knots. The sound of the wind was so loud you couldn't even communicate with people, and I knew if anyone went over, there was just no chance. At that point, I really didn't know if we were going to survive.

Q: So would you say it was like a near death experience?

LARRY: It probably was. This went on for several hours; it was quite frightening.

Q: Do you think this experience influenced your market behavior in any way?

LARRY: Perhaps it made me feel more humble or maybe more mortal.

Q: Well, has that affected your approach to risk?

LARRY: What seriously affected my approach is of a very personal nature: my first wife's death. I understood real hardship. It put the "life and death" of trading in perspective. I mean, you know, you lose some money, so what? You lose someone you love, that's pretty serious stuff. It made me stop taking trading so seriously.

Q: In what way?

LARRY: Well, dollars and sense. I mean, you hear it all the time, maybe it's trite, but it's true. If you have your health, you've got everything. Traders tend to confuse trading with life.

Q: Jeff Silverman said something really interesting when I interviewed him. As you know, he's been very successful in the markets. He said he actually didn't do well at trading until he got to a point where he didn't give a hoot about the money.

LARRY: Well, that's right. He's not trading dollars.

Q: To what extent do you believe your personal understanding of risk contributed to your success as a trader?

LARRY: Well, I think appreciating risk, being aware of it and respecting it, makes you a good trader. It teaches you to be disciplined.

Discipline allows you to trade effectively. You can take your ego out of it. You can be wrong 60, 70 percent of the time and still make a lot of money. If you ignore the discipline of managing risk, you have to be right 80 percent of the time or more, and I don't know anyone who's that good. I've been around a long time. I have never seen anyone who can be right eight out of ten times. Once you realize you only have to be right 40 or 50 percent of the time with good risk management, your account starts to grow.

Q: Do you think understanding risk has anything to do with anxiety management?

LARRY: It certainly does.

Q: You said earlier that you've come to rely on the fact that you know where your risk is going in every trade.

LARRY: Absolutely.

Q: So that must take away a lot of the anxiety.

LARRY: When I first came off the floor, and I really had no technical method, I was just trying to figure out how to get into the market. I'd sit here and watch every tick and try to get my stop in. Now I make the trade, put the stop in, and I go about my business. I don't care and I don't labor over it. They either get me or they don't.

Q: Basically, everything you've said has been aimed at developing a concept of risk and circumscribing or disciplining yourself to understand the risk. This has enabled you to manage anxiety. It's what separates you today from that kid who bid on the 50 lot in corn and felt nervous.

LARRY: It's the old thing. You need to eliminate the fear of the unknown. If you don't have perimeters, that's an unknown. I mean, if I have a position that closes against me, and I'm not sure where to get out, and tomorrow the market opens against me, well, now I'm trying to figure it out while the bullets are flying. I want my game plan worked out before the shooting starts. Otherwise, it's too late.

Q: So disciplining yourself to minimize the risk helps you deal with the unknown, right?

LARRY: Yes. First I establish the risk. And I know the worst-case scenario. Then the risk can only be good. I know it's all up-side after that.

Q: What advice can you give traders about understanding risk in order to optimize their trading performance?

LARRY: Just what I've been saying. You have to determine your risk reward going into a trade and place that stop. Have that risk limit and keep it. The mistake people make is that they establish their risk. They say, okay, I'm going to get out at point X. Then the market gets a little close and they'll move their stop. In my judgment that's a cardinal sin, and that's lesson 101.

Q: When it came to understanding risk, what did you learn most about yourself?

LARRY: That I'm fallible and that I personally made all the mistakes I've cautioned your readers to be aware of. You know, Howard, you need to realize in trading, as in life, every lesson you pay for. No one gets a scholarship. There is a price for real understanding. It's tuition. That's one thing for sure, after 30 years, I've figured out.

8

David Silverman

David Silverman is a long-time member of the Chicago Mercantile Exchange. He was an active floor trader in the currency pits and is currently serving as a member of the exchange's board of directors. He is also a partner in M&S Trading, a commodities trading adviser. David holds a BA with honors in history from the University of Chicago.

Q: David, what first attracted you to the area of speculation?

DAVID: I was in law school, and I didn't like it very much. My father was involved in trading through a partner of his who had come down and set up an operation in the 1970s to clear trades. My dad introduced me to his partner, and I began working as a clerk on the floor. After doing this for four summers, I learned a lot about the markets. When I decided that I didn't want to be a lawyer, trading seemed like a natural thing for me to do. In the late seventies and early eighties, there were a lot of opportunities on the trading floor. The markets were growing exponentially, and it was relatively inexpensive to get started. I started trading with $5,000 in my account, which I borrowed from my dad. Today, in 1997, $5,000 doesn't even take you far at Starbucks.

Q: What was it specifically about trading that attracted you?

DAVID: The first minute that I stepped on the trading floor in the summer of 1978, I was hooked. I remember when my dad sent me down here; the job paid minimum wage, and it wasn't even a full day's work because the markets were open less than eight hours. I just loved it. The noise, the cast of characters, the activity—there was just so much going on. It was scary, but it was very exciting, too. And there were a lot of young people on the floor. It was a vital place. It seemed like a place where I might be able to get involved and do very well for myself. I also knew that if it didn't pan out, I could always go back to the law. Keep in mind, though, when I walked into my first civil procedure class, I didn't have that same visceral feeling of excitement that I did when I first walked on the exchange floor.

Q: Do you believe that what first interested you in trading still holds the same attraction?

DAVID: Not at all. The trading floor has grown and the participants—and I include myself—have gotten older and less exciting, I suppose. But it's not the superficial part that excites me anymore. I think that over the years I developed an understanding of what it is that really makes the markets attractive to people, and that's the fact that if you're smart and disciplined, and if you manage your risk properly, you can make a great deal of money. It's not easy for people who are outside of the industry to understand that. They just see, as I did when I walked on the floor for the first time, the superficial part of it—the noise, the arms flying back and forth, and the high flyers. They assume that it must somehow be like a great big casino where every time a trader makes a bet, he's throwing a $1,000 chip on the table. I think that when you have a more sophisticated understanding of what's going on, you recognize that the traders who are extremely successful are ones who are putting their chips down on the table in a very measured, sophisticated way. I think that the casino analogy might, on its surface, seem a negative comparison, but it's actually an apt analogy for successful trading in the sense that if you understand how odds work, and if you make bets that are appropriate to the stake that you start out with, you probably will walk away from the table a winner. If you're just going to buy a hundred-dollar bag of coins and put them in a big slot machine just for the kick of it, you could win or lose, but in the long run, you will definitely lose. There is no question about that. If you are playing blackjack and double down every time you get aces and don't put everything down on one hand, there's a reasonably good chance you'll end up walking away from the table a winner. I think that's what traders need to understand in order to be successful.

Q: What psychological biases do you think most people bring to trading that make it so difficult for them?

DAVID: I think that people naturally hate to lose, and it's not even the money so much. It's the depression, the anxiety, the lack of ability to deal with not always being right that makes it so difficult. I remember reading a long time ago about a model that a CTA had tested, and it went back like 20 years on ten different markets, but generated enough trades to be statistically significant. The system was actually quite successful, and it's not really important what the system was except to say that at some point in the series of trades that were tested, they found that there were 14 consecutive losers. Over time the system made lots of money. It was a successful system. But most of the people that I know who trade can barely recover from losing two or three times in a row, much less 14! So, I think that you find that people who are the most successful at this are the ones that have enough self-confidence to understand that if their system is robust and intellectually sound, and coupled with strong risk management techniques, they can afford to wait out 14 consecutive losing trades. Again, most traders are going to have a hard time losing 14 times in a row, but the best traders do it. They know that there's probably going to be a period where they will make money 14 times in a row, and because they've managed their risk properly and not blown their stake during that losing streak, they're going to be around to reap the benefits of their robust system.

Q: David, what personal prejudices relevant to managing risk do you believe you had to wrestle with in order to effect a successful result in your trading?

DAVID: When I was younger, it was much easier for me to deal with losses because I had far fewer responsibilities. I didn't have the four children I have now. I wasn't married, and I really felt that if something bad happened, I would recover from it. It was just me, and I was young enough to cope with it. As I've gotten older, I've become more averse to taking risks, and I believe that can be seen as a good thing and a bad thing. In truth, I don't know that I ever took any untoward risks, risks that would put me out of the business even when I was younger. But I think currently my risk antennae are up all the time now. I tend to put myself in positions where it's really hard to believe that any one thing that I am going to do is going to place me in an impossible situation. And I think that's a good thing. If you're not always hitting home runs, you can still make a lot of money going for singles and doubles. When I was less risk averse, I was more apt to hit a home run, and now that I'm more risk averse, I'm probably hitting a lot more singles and doubles, but that's just fine. It's hard to lose, and, you know, it's easy to sit and give an interview and say that people should have confidence in their system. But I'm not immune to those feelings and, yes, my personal prejudices. I think I tend to lose self-confidence if I have a streak where things aren't going well. And I just try and pull myself out of it, slowly. If I had 14 losing trades in a row, I wouldn't try and make it all back on the 15th. I think actually I'm quite good at that. I recognize that someone who tries to do that is generally heading towards trouble.

Q: How do you actually deal with the question of uncertainty?

DAVID: I try to study the markets constantly, no matter whether I'm doing well or poorly. I always think I'm on top of what's going on in the market. I generally know where the major chart points are, when the reports are coming out, and I know what is the market expectation. And I talk every day to people who have other ideas about the market than I do just to test out my point of view.

Q: So you're saying preparation.

DAVID: Preparation is one way I deal with uncertainty. Today, for instance, December 5, is an unemployment day, and the number that came out was radically different than what was expected. Knowing that—the time when they release the number—gives you a leg up on someone who doesn't have that information. So to answer your question, preparation is one thing that helps me deal with uncertainty. If nothing else, preparation gives me a knowledge base about the market so I don't sit around beating myself up that I'm such an idiot. I have a couple of colleagues who I'm close with. We're very supportive of each other. When I'm doing poorly, I think they help support me, and I provide the same sort of comfort when they're doing poorly. I think it helps to have peers that you respect and with whom you can discuss what's going on, both in the market and your personal trading. But when it comes down to it, I think dealing with uncertainty is ultimately a function of how self-confident you are. You can talk to every trader on the exchange floor, but when it comes down to it, it's you who has to pull the trigger. It's you who has to get a statement the next morning. The point is, in the final analysis it's up to you to trade confidently, and if you don't feel you can do that, then you shouldn't be trading.

Q: How do you deal with not being in control of the market?

DAVID: Howard, that's a good question. I've had arguments with other traders about this very issue. Friends of mine who are much bigger traders sometimes think that they can go for short periods of time and actually control the market. You know, let's say bull a market! If you go over to the Board of Trade, and you watch some of the larger traders, a guy like Tom Baldwin in the bonds, he tends to be the biggest player in the biggest market around, and it seems on the surface that he can bull the market. Personally, I have never felt like those guys, and certainly not myself, a much smaller trader, ever had control over the market, even for one second. It's ironic, isn't it? We're sitting in the offices at Rand Financial Futures, named after the author Ayn Rand, who would be turning over in her grave if she thought that anyone could control the market. The market's bigger than all of us, and I think anyone who thinks they can control the market is living in a fantasy world. But I think that the fact that you don't have control over the market doesn't mean that you don't have control over what you do in the market. There's a big distinction there. It's not subtle or semantic. In order to trade successfully, you have to accept that the market's bigger than you are, but within the scope of what's happening, there are huge opportunities. Remember, everybody else who's participating in the market is subject to the control of the market, so the fact that none of us control the market is really irrelevant to me as long I'm in control of myself.

Q: David, how do you deal with taking a loss?

DAVID: I think I deal very well with taking losses. I think that may be a function of not looking to hit home runs all the time, but maybe it's more than that. I think it's just that I recognize that I can be wrong and still make a lot of money. From the beginning of my trading career, it's never been a real big problem for me to take a loss. I think that the only time I've ever experienced real anxiety about losses is to the extent that it inhibits my ability to take a profit. What I mean by that is that if I'm long the market and it's rallying and I get out, I'm uncomfortable when it continues rallying. So I've recognized a profit, and in some sense was right the market, but by taking a profit I've let the market take my money. Of course, it's very easy to rectify this situation by simply getting back in the market. So maybe my loss is only the difference between where I got out of the market and where I got back in. However, many times I divorce myself from the position; it's generally not easy for me to get back in the market, and that's because I wouldn't have gotten out in the first place if I weren't uncomfortable with the fear of losing. So, I think the only time I get upset about loss is when I get out of the market too soon and I don't let my profits run. That's a much bigger problem for me than sticking with a losing position for days and days.

Q: How do you calculate risk?

DAVID: My definitions for calculating risk have evolved over time, as my trading styles have changed. When I first began, I was a scalper, pure and simple. I tried to buy the bid and sell the offer. In the eighties and even the early nineties, when there was a lot of retail business coming into the foreign currencies where I trade, that was a pretty simple thing to do. It became more difficult as the market became more sophisticated, more institution oriented. The moves tended to be extreme and happened in many cases overnight, not during the U.S. trading hours when I was trading. So I had to develop the ability to trade differently, to trade positions rather than just scalp for a few ticks here and there. As a scalper, I would define risk very simply: If I were long and the market went against me I would get out at the next lower offer. Generally, the market was thick enough that being wrong only cost a tick or two at a time. And it depended on how big a position I had on; usually it was hundreds of contracts and that translated to just a few thousand dollars per tick. I always felt that was reasonable, given the account size I had. As my trading style has changed, I've begun to look more toward bigger market moves. At the same time, Peter Mulmat and I opened up a firm to manage customer money, and we began to look at risk in a much more systematic way. We looked at the amount of money that we had under management and adopted the basic premise that we never wanted to lose more than 1 or 2 percent of the money under management on any individual trade. It was quite simple then to figure out exactly how many contracts we had on. If we had $1 million under management and we believed that the deutsche mark might be making a 160-point move over the next week, we were willing to put in a 40-point stop, and just multiply that by 20 contracts to establish our maximum risk scenario. Without going into too many details, there were times where we might ratchet it up to 2 percent, but the point is that we never wanted to lose more than 1 to 2 percent of the money under management on any individual trade. And the idea behind that was that we may have been wrong a number of times in a row, but that at 1 or 2 percent per time, we weren't going to get blown out.

Q: David, according to your understanding of risk, are risk management and money management the same thing?

DAVID: Yes. I don't know that I understood that when I started trading, but I think that you can't divorce the one from the other. I think if you divorce the two, you're kidding yourself or you're looking for trouble. Because when it comes down to it, you need to be able to have the ability to lose, and strong risk management techniques, coupled with a strong money management program, give you the ability to lose. If you don't have strong risk management, you don't have money management. Otherwise it's just gambling. I know a lot of traders who are successful and have been successful for a long time who actually don't understand that risk management is the same as good money management. Now, that's not to say that every trader who's successful has some mathematical formula or model of risk. It may be intuitive. If you go down into the S&P pit right now with all the volatility they've had, where I think the average daily range was something like $12,000 a contract during 1997, there are traders who trade 50 and 100 contracts at a crack; I mean, the numbers are astounding, and you wondered whether these guys had millions of dollars in their accounts that they could justify these sorts of positions. But they have some sort of intuitive mechanism, I think, that equates to someone else's mathematical model. They wouldn't be able to continue doing this day after day for all these years without some sort of concept of risk management. So I can't divorce them. Maybe someone else can, but for me the two concepts go in tandem.

Q: What do you think is the riskiest thing you've ever done or experienced in your life?

DAVID: Trading!

Q: Really, what was the riskiest trade?

DAVID: I think the riskiest trade I ever made was in the Canadian dollar. A buyer came into the market and wanted to buy the equivalent of about $500 million Canadian. It was something like 5,000 contracts. And they were willing to pay a premium to fill this order. It was Friday, and it was late in the day, and I was one of the few people in the pit. It was what you might call a slam dunk trade for some enormous money. And I experienced the adrenaline flowing—my eyes were wide, and I knew I could have had a large part of this trade if not the entire thing. In many ways it felt like the trade of a lifetime. I'm still talking about it years later, and I didn't take it. I took about 10 percent of the trade, 500 contracts. And the thing is, even though I'm talking about it years later, and even though I still beat myself up because I didn't take the whole 5,000 lot (because I made a lot of money on the 500 lot and it would have been ten times more) I know I did the right thing. You know, Howard, even though it seems like a slam dunk, even Michael Jordan misses a slam dunk! Every now and then, and I'm not Michael Jordan, you don't want to be on the wrong side of a $500 million Canadian order, especially late on a Friday just before the market closes. And so, even though I beat myself up years later that I didn't make what I should have on this trade, I had plenty of risk with 500 contracts on, and it turned out well for me. But if it had not turned out well, if it hadn't been a slam dunk on the 500, I still could have come back on Monday morning. And that was probably the riskiest trade I ever made, but like I said it turned out well. I spent the weekend shaking, but I came back Monday morning.

Q: How has that experience influenced your market behavior subsequently?

DAVID: Actually, I don't know that that specific trade influenced my market behavior. But in looking back at it, and knowing that, given the same situation, I would do the same thing, I think that it shows that a disciplined approach is inculcated in my way of thinking. And you know what? The fact of the matter is that there are probably some successful traders on the floor who would have taken the whole 5,000 contracts. And I'm not sure they would have been wrong; but at least for me, I did the right thing. I think that in general this disciplined approach has allowed me to be successful. When you start making compromises or coming up with rationalizations why this situation is different, that's when you start getting yourself in trouble.

Q: I have a feeling that success, in this instance or in most instances, is staying true to who you are, and that those people who might have taken the whole 5,000-contract order would have been very comfortable, because that's who they are.

DAVID: Right.

Q: And you stayed within your personal definition of disciplined trading.

DAVID: Right.

Q: And that's the secret of success in this business.

DAVID: Right. I think you hit the nail on the head. Because someone who would have taken that 5,000 and really couldn't handle it might have made money on that trade, but the next time something came along they would get run over. So, I think you're right. For me, I did the right thing, and I think it was just a pattern of behavior that developed over the years and will continue to serve me well.

Q: To what extent do you believe your personal understanding of risk contributes to your success as a trader?

DAVID: I don't think that I would have been able to trade successfully over the years without first an intuitive understanding of risk and then later a more systematic, if you will, mathematical understanding of risk.

Q: How has it affected your motivation for trading?

DAVID: It's actually made it a lot easier. I mean, knowing what you're going to do before you do it, having some rules govern your activity, really makes life a lot easier. It makes being disciplined not a hard thing. Some people look at being disciplined and say, how am I going to do that? But the other side of the coin is that when you know you have to do something a certain way, there's really a lot fewer decisions to make. You don't have to beat yourself up as long as you follow what you know is right.

Q: How has it affected your beliefs about yourself in the market?

DAVID: Again, I think that it's made it a lot easier for me to function.

Q: Does that include anxiety management?

DAVID: Yes. But I'm not saying I never get anxious.

Q: Well, we all do.

DAVID: And I'm not saying I never break the discipline. You know, I wish I was that disciplined, that I was perfect. But if nothing else, at least when I break out of a discipline pattern, I understand exactly what I've done. When I sit down and analyze it—and I do try and analyze what I'm doing—I can see where I made mistakes.

Q: What advice can you give traders about understanding risk in order to optimize their trading performance?

DAVID: I've known a million traders, and every single one of them who's made money has had a way that's different than mine. You know, there may be some threads running through that are the same, but essentially I think that there are as many different ways to make money as there are traders. Having said that, I would also say that every trader has to develop his or her own risk management model. Some people are going to be very risk averse, while some people are going to be more aggressive. There's nothing wrong with that. Being cognizant of risk management doesn't mean that you can't be aggressive, nor does it mean that you shouldn't be risk averse; it just means profoundly understanding what it is that you're looking for and trying to come up with, either on an intuitive or systematic basis.

Q: Do you think traders can succeed at trading if they don't understand how to calculate and manage risk?

DAVID: No, I don't think so.

Q: Why not?

DAVID: I think that if they don't understand risk, they'll get blown out. I remember when I first started out I was clueless. I'd gone to the University of Chicago where I got straight As, but when I came to the exchange, for about a year and a half I could barely make a winning trade. I didn't know what was going on. And I remember I was searching for some method that would allow me to succeed at trading. Like many novice traders, I was looking for some easy way to make money. I remember hearing about this system called the congestion system, and I remember trying to block it out of my memory for reasons you'll understand in a minute. I think the key part of the system was that if you had three up closes in a row, you would sell the market, and on the next day, you would cover your position. If you had three downs, you would buy it and so on. There were about thirty other patterns, and it was supposed to govern just about anything that could happen in the market. I bought into this because I wanted to buy into it! The first trade I made, I remember I sold the deutsche mark after it had closed up three times in a row; it opened, I don't know, about 80 or 90 points to where I made $1,000 per contract. Well, I had found the Holy Grail of trading, the magnificent congestion system. I lost that $1,000 and many thousands more before I finally gave it up and realized that I had to come up with my own ideas. So, you can convince yourself that there's some easy methodology that's not going to require you to know what's going on. But if that's the case, you probably should just take your money and give it to a money manager. There are a lot of good ones out there. If you want to trade, you have to develop your own ideas.

Q: When it came to understanding risk, what did you learn most about yourself?

DAVID: I learned that I was capable of disciplining myself. I learned that the so-called easy way to do things was really to discipline myself rather than to try and make a lot of money. And this congestion system that I spoke of is a perfect example of what I'm talking about. It really takes a lot of hard personal work to develop into a winning trader, not just a system. Once I recognized that it was important to do that hard personal work, I learned that I could be a successful trader.

9

Larry Carr

Larry Carr is a long-time member of the Chicago Board of Trade. He is an active independent trader.

Q: Larry, what first attracted you to the area of speculation?

LARRY: I started when I was six years old. My father had some farm animals that he gave me. We sold them for $140 and with the proceeds bought 20 shares of National Airlines. I enjoyed following the stock; it gave me something to do and kept me out of my dad's hair while he was watching the ticker tapes at his broker's office. All through grade school I traded stock, and I also used to trade coins. Looking back, there was always a trader in me, trading different things—even baseball cards.

Q: What specifically did you find interesting?

LARRY: Initially, it was just to see how much I could make. I guess it was the accumulation of assets or something. I remember that I always wanted to trade coins, to buy something a little cheaper and try to sell it a little better. I was always looking for the best deal; it was a way that I learned how to develop a concept about the value of things. My father was kind of a long-term value-oriented guy. He would see something that looked bad, but believed that it would turn around and increase in value. He held out for the long term. Of course, some things he bought kept on going down. When I started trading commodities I had to start developing my own ideas about value and price. The first two trades I ever made, I bought sugar at 10 percent off the contract highs and sold it 10 percent off the contract low. I lost half the money I had.

Q: That's not an uncommon story for an initial speculation in the futures market.

LARRY: I also used to play poker 30 hours a week.

Q: You like gambling games then.

LARRY: I don't particularly, but I did it to make money.

Q: Were you a successful gambler?

LARRY: Yes. I wasn't a high-stakes guy, but I had a very good conservative game. I wasn't a genius at it, but if I stuck to my simple rules I did okay.

Q: Larry, do you think that what first attracted you to trading still holds the same appeal?

LARRY: Yes, I do. Because since my initial trades that I mentioned a moment ago I'm always trying to do the best I can. I'm trying to safeguard my assets and improve my approach. At times, I feel like I should be a little looser in my ways. Hopefully, I'll be able to be that someday. It's a project that I have to work on. Now that my cash position is better I have more money to risk, but I'm still pretty conservative. I look for the trade where everything lines up for me, and it seems like lately those trades really don't make as much money. The ones that make the money are the dumpy ones that involve more risk and I'm really not that sure of.

I constantly try to have good risk reward on any trade, but after, it seems like I make most of my money on trades that have poor risk reward. In truth I have such a high percentage of hitting that I don't get hurt that often on those trades, which is amazing. But also, it's always hard for me to put any size on these trades, because I'm afraid of exposing myself to unnecessary risk.

Q: But the percentage of winners that you get out of these trades is very good.

LARRY: Yes.

Q: Well then, that's a legitimate exercise in choosing trades. If they're high-percentage trades, you can afford to give up more on the risk side. Larry, what natural psychological biases do you feel most people bring to trading that makes it so difficult?

LARRY: Fear that they may be wrong. If the trade is no good, don't hang around. Don't stay with the losers. Get out and start over again!

Q: Did you have to wrestle with that?

LARRY: Initially I did. As I mentioned earlier, I had that sugar position, and I lost half my money. It was four months of agony. I can remember going up to my broker's office with a check. "Here's 3,000 more dollars." So, to answer your question, Howard, it was something that I had to learn to cope with.

I think I bought some tapes, and I used to say some affirmations about getting out of every loser. And I wrote up something that was designed to remind me to cut my losses. When I came up to Chicago to become a floor trader they kind of reiterated that same thing, "get rid of your losers, and just get out." And of course, "try to hold onto your winners." So for the last 20 years, that's what I've been trying to do

Q: How do you deal with the issue of uncertainty?

LARRY: I write out what I believe the market scenario will be for any given day. I'll address a number of different issues. If I think today is going to be a normal trading day, then this is what I believe should be the normal range. Therefore I have established a way to look at the market with broad perspective, eliminating the emotion. So if the scenario that I have constructed begins to unfold, then I just start playing my numbers. I find this approach works out pretty well. One issue I still find myself wrestling with is that at times I do watch the screen too much. Consequently, I'll buy and sell from time to time at low-volume areas in the market and I won't get the follow-through that I'm anticipating.

Q: Larry, you have been a market maker on the floor of the Chicago Board of Trade for many years and undoubtedly understand the risk and reward ratios required of a pit trader. How has making the transition to an upstairs trader affected your understanding of risk management?

LARRY: I find being off the floor makes me more conservative in my approach. I find myself being much more protective of profits. In fact, to a certain extent being off the floor closes up my trading a bit.

Q: Your trading gets closed because you're away from the floor?

LARRY: Yes, I'm more risk averse than I was in the pit.

Q: Why do you think that is?

LARRY: Maybe just to protect my profits. I don't know if it's my ego . . .

Q: You know Larry, I can relate to this in personal terms. When I was in the pit, I would feel that with any position I had on I could get out very easily due to my proximity to the action. I felt my escape route was close by and immediate, and when I had to move out of a bad position I could do it instantaneously. Is that true of your experience?

LARRY: Yes, very much so.

Q: So being upstairs has changed your perception of risk control. Is that true?

LARRY: Well, it shouldn't, you know. But I do find myself going back to what I did ten years ago. I start cutting back size. If I buy 30 contracts of beans I find myself only risking $2,000, whereas if I was trading more open I could increase my risk to $4,000 to $5,000 given my risk/reward ratios. Howard, this obviously is an issue I'm still working on. For example, this month I'm currently up twelve to fourteen thousand almost exclusively on "small" trades. If I had played it a bit more open, with increased risk I could have a much better month. But for some reason, I'm afraid of changing my approach.

Q: What are you afraid of?

LARRY: I'm afraid of getting smacked for a $50,000 or $100,000 loss on any trade. I had months scalping on the floor where I made $80,000 or $90,000. But now, trading off the floor, maybe there's a guilt associated with the fear. I know that the best thing for me is to maintain a relaxed attitude, not to get too excited or aggressive. Have things come to you on your own terms, just be mentally and physically calm . . . you know, don't get uptight, or try to make a hard decision. Because, you don't need to. I mean, in trading things will come in their own time.

Q: So is it an issue of control for you? That you're having a difficult time trying to control what you're doing in the market like you did when you used to be in the pit?

LARRY: I'm not sure, because when I was in the pit and I would be scalping 50 lots, I'd say to myself, "If I don't put a stop in, I'm going to get out at two cents above my exit point." Suddenly you've turned a small loss into a big one. So I always make it a habit, even as a floor trader, to have my stops on paper in the pit. I mean, after getting caught a couple of times over the years, I learned how important that kind of control is for a successful result.

You see, Howard, before I learned the importance of stops it would scare me. I'd come home, and I'd think, "Boy Larry, you're just out of control! You know what your game plan is and yet you can't follow it."

Q: How do you take a loss?

LARRY: I just have a stop in, and when I'm wrong the market takes me out.

Q: How do you feel about taking a loss?

LARRY: I guess, in general I would have to say I'm okay when it comes to defining and taking a market loss. And I always feel better if the trade that stops me out continues in that direction. It always bugs me, as it does everyone, when the market goes right to your stop point and turns around. As an example, the other day I sold the long bond at 115.28, risking 10 ticks. Accordingly, I placed my stop at 116.08. The market traded through my price and I was filled at 116.08. Then the market reversed dramatically and continued to sell off for 50 points. I thought, boy, maybe I shouldn't have had a stop in there! But then again the market could just as easily and rapidly have moved 50 points the other way. So again, I can't just be sitting here hoping for a better place to exit a losing position. I have to have that stop in order to control myself.

Q: You wrestle with this every day?

LARRY: Yes. It's something I think many successful traders continue to wrestle with. Today in the S&Ps I felt I should have put a larger stop in. But yesterday in the beans I bought the market at 697 on the opening, rode them up to 704½, put my stop in at breakeven; I got stopped out and it didn't bother me at all. I remember attending a seminar that Tom Baldwin was giving at the Chicago Board of Trade. He said one of the most important things that has helped my trading: You must know your time frame. Once you know your time frame, the rest of trading is playing chess. Howard, I'm not a fast guy; I'm more of a slow guy who uses a three-day period. Beyond that, I don't have a clue about what's going on. The psychologist Van Tharpe once asked me to pick an animal that most personified me. Most traders come up with panthers or cheetahs; a lot of traders picked tigers. They would see the trade setting up and jump on it. Well, I told him that I felt like I was a guernsey cow, out on the side of a meadow chewing his cud. I'm just out there looking over the scenery trying to make sense of the landscape. That is why I say I'm not looking to pounce on the 5- or 30-minute price changes in the market. I'm looking more at the near term price wings, which I think are significant, like your approach in *The Day Trader's Advantage.* I almost feel as though this approach is a reflection of my life because it allows me to stay close with, for example, my son. He gets off the school bus from going to kindergarten. He comes in and he jumps in my arms. I mean, it's kind of like one of those times I want to be able to appreciate. I don't want to get hung up on every two-minute move in the market.

Q: Larry, how do you calculate risk? Do you have a mathematical calculation, or is it more intuitive?

LARRY: I'm going to have to say it is more a natural feel. I would like to think that I know my exit point exactly on every trade with a definite reason. And therefore, in the S&Ps, for example, I usually will be risking five points. In reality it never works out exactly that way. I mean, as soon as the market goes 200 points in my direction, I'll place my stop at breakeven. And if something like volume, for instance, does not look right to me I'll get out. But I always have my maximum stop loss in the market so that I don't get clipped or caught in market blowoffs. I am good in exiting when the market blows off in my direction.

Q: When it climaxes?

LARRY: Yes, the climaxes. I rarely, if ever, buy into those scenarios, but I use them effectively, I believe, to manage my risk when my position is on the right side of the market.

Q: Of course there are not a lot of times in the market when it will give you enough push to the upside so that you will be right buying rallies and selling breaks. How do you distinguish risk management from money management?

LARRY: I think they should be the same, but I think that I don't treat them the same. Money management, I guess, is like the whole spectrum, whereas risk management refers to the risk/reward ratio on any given trade, what you are willing to risk in this moment in time. The risk management involves the trade in the particular time frame.

Q: Whereas, according to your perspective, money management refers to the overall game plan.

LARRY: That's exactly right. It's more of the entire chess game over time.

Q: So according to you there is a difference.

LARRY: Yes. Money management is just a multiple of risk management. You're taking a series of high-probability trades, one by one over a long time horizon, and that should come out for you over the long haul.

Q: But that means you have a series of losses too, 40 to 50 percent of the time.

LARRY: Right, but if your money management is right, then you should be okay.

Q: What do you think is the riskiest thing you've ever done or experienced in your life?

LARRY: I can't really think of anything.

Q: Have you ever jumped out of an airplane?

LARRY: No. I've gone parasailing, but it really wasn't very risky. Maybe borrowing money to buy my seat on the Board of Trade.

Q: How did you feel about going into debt to go into a speculative business?

LARRY: At first it really bothered me, but I also knew down deep that it was the right thing to do. In a way I felt as if it was my destiny or something.

Q: You were comfortable with that?

LARRY: As comfortable as I could be. I was very attracted, as I said earlier, to the whole idea of speculation.

Q: Larry, has the reward been worth the risk?

LARRY: It has been the most rewarding thing I've ever done in my life.

Q: Rewarding in what sense?

LARRY: Well, my lifestyle; to be able to enjoy what I like to do. I mean, it was a big risk for me, yet I've accomplished a lot. I paid off all my debts and I was able to create this lifestyle—the life that I wanted to have for myself and my family. But again, looking back, it was a very scary thing!

Q: To what extent do you believe the way you understand risk contributes to your success as a trader?

LARRY: It's essential. If you don't understand risk you will not be able to establish trading goals. You will be out of control all the time. Without an understanding of calculated risk, everything in the trading process is too wild and crazy. I've always said to myself that if I followed five principles I would become the best trader I could be. Be the best human being, which means be the best father and husband. Be healthy, vibrant, and in great shape; and stick to my risk management system. If I do all these things I'll be the best trader that I can be.

You know, Howard, my understanding of risk is greatly tied to my personal belief system. When I enter into a marketplace, I can't do what a Richard Dennis or a Tom Baldwin does. I have to know what my little niche is. That's where I have market certainty and control. I am always looking to capture some control over my little territory, when I can manage exactly what it is that I'm doing. I am a creature of habit. When I see familiar patterns or price movement, I really believe I can project what is going to happen. I have seen it so many times in the past and have been able to exploit those situations. So I guess to a large degree it is intuitive. I look to take advantage of analogs that seem reliable based on my previous market experience.

Q: How do you manage your anxiety?

LARRY: I run, and I do exercise. I also try to watch out that I'm not being too intense. I just try to stay psychologically relaxed and focused. And additionally, I always keep my stops in. Especially on one lots. You know, it's always the one lots that will kill you! I was going home one day from the exchange, and my quotron, which works on an FM band, was not coming in. It works alright for about 25 miles, but occasionally I lose my signal. So I lost it for about 10 or 15 minutes, and when it came back I found that I had lost 1,000 points in the S&P. It was only one contract, but as I said before, the risk on that one-lot S&P can be significant.

Q: Larry, what advice would you give traders about understanding risk in order to optimize their trading performance?

LARRY: Just know yourself and know what you're looking for and at in the market. Also, be consistent, as I said earlier, about sticking to a specific time frame

Q: When it comes to understanding risk, what have you learned most about yourself?

LARRY: I've learned that I have to be myself and stick to my own personal beliefs and principles. I know if I'm just consistent with my own approach, carefully calculating acceptable risk and staying mentally relaxed, the trading discipline and profits will just naturally follow. I've also learned that I need defined goals and a projected scenario within my time frame. The rest is just playing chess.

10

Tom Grossman

Tom Grossman is president of SAC International Equities, LLC. He was formerly the head foreign equities trading strategist for Kingdon Capital Management.

Q: Tom, what first attracted you to the area of speculation?

TOM: I think it was the immediacy of the trading environment, the way that the market taught you lessons and gave you feedback as to the validity of what you were doing. You could go home at the end of the day and have a P&L that would tell you how you had done that day.

Q: Were there any early experiences in your life that you feel led you into a trading career?

TOM: My father was a gambler. I had gone to the racetrack all my life, and I learned about and understood probabilities and fear and greed. In gambling there are many of the same aspects that make trading so interesting.

Q: Do you believe that the same things that interested you in trading initially hold the same attraction today?

TOM: Yes, although I think it's expanded quite a bit. I view my trading much more as an evolutionary process. It's something that's going to be with me for a long time, and I'm going to get better and better at it. I don't view it so much as maximizing each hour's or each day's profits. But in general, the same things that attracted me early on still attract me now.

Q: Does that include a feeling of excitement?

TOM: I think over time the excitement has become less compelling. Clearly, it was a lot of the attraction at the beginning—the jolt of electricity that you got when you held a position. Over time, the survival skills of trading teach you that you can't get that up when things are going well, and you can't get that down when things are going poorly. When you're trading, the less emotional you get the better. However, the emotion for seeking out the angle and getting an edge on the market is greater today than it was in the past. So I'd say, at different parts of the trading process, the rush or excitement is still important today.

Q: Tom, how does seeking market advantage or getting an edge manifest itself in your trading?

TOM: It manifests itself now in monitoring a wide variety of asset classes in a wide geographical region. Having a large catalog of prior experiences lets me apply knowledge that I acquired in trading—for example, in Korea five years ago or in Argentina today. I think it's the past experience, the contacts and ability to monitor a very wide variety of tradable securities across product lines in different geographical regions—applying knowledge in a very nontraditional way.

Q: What personal prejudices do you think you had to wrestle with in order to effect a successful result in your own trading?

TOM: I think to trade effectively I had to get over an uncomfortableness with expecting to be extremely successful. By that, I mean I had to constantly check my feeling that I had such an advantage over the market that I must have been missing something. Because of it, I let many opportunities slip by. So I had to really gain the confidence in myself and my own judgment. Luckily, in my career I had been given very good exposure to a lot of different investors. So this experience, coupled with a willingness to trade areas that were not easily traded, where there were no established algorithms, placed me in a unique position to consistently have an advantage in the market. I just had to get comfortable with my own assessment of opportunity.

I think I had to wrestle with this feeling of inner arrogance, if you will—to really step up when you're right and take a big swing. The personal prejudices with me and with most people are a fear to bet too much in any one situation. You don't want to leave yourself exposed to too much drawdown, which in general is a very good rule. But in my view, risk is a two-edged sword, and sometimes the risk is in not making enough when you're right. If you view your trading as a long-term process, then you're going to be wrong a lot. Lord knows I'm wrong a ton. Sometimes, in a very perverse way, the risk to me becomes not having a big enough bet when I really had all the cards and I was right!

Q: Can you describe a recent event that would illustrate this?

TOM: Sure, a recent trade we made in Telcom ITO. We bought it at 11.80 and it went straight down. Investors weren't really viewing the stock in a global context as I did. It's a cellular phone stock in China, and I viewed it as I would a cellular phone stock in Sweden, the U.S., Korea, India. I thought I truly understood what was going on in a way the market at large didn't. The stock went down, but I had the guts to really sit there and say, yes, it's down, and yes, by some mechanistic model, I would have to say I was wrong and sell out. But I felt I understood why it was down, and I thought I had a good view as to what would change. I bought more stock as it went lower and it turned out to be a very, very profitable trade.

Q: You thought the market was good and purchased it for 11.80 Hong Kong dollars?

TOM: Right. When I committed to buy it I thought the market was good, so we purchased it. In the meantime, some factors completely unrelated to this specific security panicked international investors into selling it down into the $9 range. And you know, we weren't stupid about it. We waited to watch it bottom a little bit and find a level. We thought the worst case was already built into the price, and so we had to buy a lot more. And again, the risk on this trade once it went down was not owning enough, in my opinion.

Q: And how did you hedge the market risk?

TOM: We shorted some of the bigger, more liquid stocks in the market that we thought would ultimately fall prey to a lot of the same general market concerns that had affected the initial selling of Telcom ITO. We definitely thought the market would bottom. Hong Kong has a tendency to do V bottoms and not just go flat and then up like in Mexico. So what we wanted to do was hold the stocks that we felt very comfortable with on a global basis, like a China Telcom or a China Southern Airlines. When the market turned, we could cover and then get to a net long position very quickly. This strategy worked out well.

Q: Tom, how do you formally implement risk management in your trading?

TOM: We have clear mechanistic processes that force us to ask specific questions related to risk. If the stock has a certain amount of drawdown or underperforms a local market or an industry, it's going to be called into question; we will critically analyze the situation to determine if we are wrong. We will ask ourselves, "Is the premise from which we made this trade still valid, and are we still convinced that we have an edge in this trade?" Our risk management rules force us to look at ourselves in the mirror and answer these questions.

Q: How do you deal with uncertainty?

TOM: My way of dealing with it is by being very clear with myself when entering the trade about what my expectations are. I want to know very clearly why I'm buying the stock, where I think the trade is wrong; also, what are the potential catalysts for making the market come around to my view of the situation. And as long as I think I have answers for all of these questions, I feel as though I have an edge in the position. And, of course, to be brutally honest with myself when I think that whatever I thought was going to be an edge is not an edge; I immediately get out of the position.

Q: Are there many times when you do that?

TOM: Very often—the majority of the times!

Q: How do you deal with not being in control of the market?

TOM: I've taken that as a given, and I think as long as you're prepared to take the financial drawdown and inevitable risk of the position, where the uncertainty doesn't surprise you, not being in control is absolutely expected.

For me, all I'm in control of, if I'm right, is making good trades. I have full faith that if I make enough good trades through the year that I'm going to make money. So I guess the way I deal with it, and you're helping me focus in on my own thoughts, is in having faith in my process over the long term. It makes me believe that any drawdowns are just that. So, in the last analysis, all I have to do is remain true to the process and keep placing ideas onto the assembly line.

Q: How do you deal with taking a loss?

TOM: Well, I'm working hard at embracing taking a loss and viewing it as just another learning experience. Theoretically, sitting here off the trading desk, I can tell you that's what I do, and to some extent that's what I do on the desk as well. Usually, taking a loss is cathartic—you've had a sense that it's going wrong for a little while, and you're now free. I really try to treat losses as impersonal, temporary situations, and in reality I'm thoroughly good at forgetting about them.

Q: How do you calculate risk?

TOM: In my business, risk is very difficult because all the algorithms to calculate risk are based on bad assumptions. I think that liquidity by its very nature is a discontinuous function, and it's more so in my markets. I think it's true in every market, even the most liquid markets. In recent years we have seen $2 and $3 spreads in the S&P 500 futures. You know, most models say if you're wrong it will cost 5 ticks—let's say 70 cents. But in reality you can throw that out the window! It's a discontinuous function, and at times you'd be selling them down $3, $4 in the S&Ps.

Q: Do you use that in any of your calculations for assessing risk?

TOM: Yes, I do. I basically look at worst-case scenarios. I've been involved in markets like the Korean equity market that can go limit down three or four days in a row. So, I employ a money management strategy that can tolerate that sort of event. Again, I also think the best way to manage risk is to manage the reward. You have to be able to identify significant upside potential in a market. I don't think most people do a good enough job of that. They just say that, yes, I think I can make X number of dollars in IBM.

Q: Do you think that risk management and money management are the same?

TOM: Yes, I do. I think most people use money management as an excuse not to really take a big stab at something that's a very good odds bet for them. I think for me risk management and money management are very much the same: As long as I can tolerate the dollar amount of risk that's inherent in a position, then I'm going to be comfortable with it in a drawdown. I believe it all relates to clearly establishing your expectations when you enter the trade, not changing them when you're already in the trade.

For me risk and reward really can't be separated. When there are times when the reward is judged to be so much bigger you have to be willing to assume greater risk.

Q: To what extent do you believe your personal understanding of risk contributes to your success as a trader?

TOM: I think it has everything to do with my success as a trader. I think what I view as the real risk is not in a daily mark or in a weekly mark but in getting into a situation where you're no longer able to use your investment process. I think having the confidence that you have a very good knowledge of that risk and have it under control allows you to operate in an optimal trading performance state. It allows you to capitalize on the opportunities that are out there without an undue focus. It's sort of like a chicken and an egg type of thing. If you feel confident that you have sufficient risk controls in place, then you don't have to worry about risk as much and are free to trade in a way that is optimum for you.

Q: Does it have anything to do with anxiety management?

TOM: Absolutely. The way I conquered that was in being confident, having positive expectations, which were formed on a system that I know works over the long haul.

Q: So having good risk control increases a feeling of optimism about your outcomes.

TOM: Absolutely. And I think you have to focus on positive stimulus when you're trading. You can't put risk behind you unless you truly believe that you have good controls in place. And once you do that, then you're free to focus on the positive, on the reward, on making sure you're maximizing each edge and on just feeling good about yourself and the whole process.

Q: Can you give me an example of how your understanding of risk contributes to, say, your market strategy?

TOM: Sure. When you are wrong-footed in a market and it's going against you clearly the majority of the time, and you have to sell or undo your position. If you understand how that fits into the context of your portfolio at the time, and, more importantly, into your investment process for that month or year, and really believe that you can focus on that fact, you can stay relaxed and focused on your specific market approach rather than on the fact that you're down X number of dollars.

Q: Tom, what advice would you give traders about understanding risk in order to optimize their trading performance?

TOM: I think they have to use sound money management techniques, which are available anywhere, to create a process that they believe will work over the long term. They should maintain drawdowns that are livable, viewed in the context of a month's or year's trading profits. And they really should not invest until they're very comfortable that they understand what their drawdowns are going to be and are prepared to take them; to not get a negative mental outlook when they happen. I always, even within the midst of the worst drawdown, try to focus on what the next opportunity is. Once they truly believe that they have that figured out, they can deal with whatever the market throws at them. They will have to learn how to constantly focus on the positive.

Q: Do you think that traders can succeed at trading if they don't fully understand how to calculate and evaluate risk?

TOM: No. I think to truly understand the full implications of dealing with risk you have to live in the moment, and if you're simultaneously trying to trade and emotionally deal with risk, you're dead.

Q: When it comes to understanding risk, what did you learn most about yourself?

TOM: That I am a confident, resilient person, and that if forced to, I'm prepared to do without a lot of the things that I have right now. Also, over the long haul, that I'm going to do well, and that I have to be almost religious about analyzing risk, but I don't have to fear it.

11

Scott Foster

Scott A. Foster is president and CEO of Dominion Capital Management, Inc., a trading firm that specializes in global financial derivatives with $200 million under management. Before forming DCM in 1994, Mr. Foster was senior trader for AO Management Corp. Foster holds a bachelor's degree from Grove City College, where he studied philosophy and religion. He is also a professional magician and has given presentations internationally on the relationship between trading and perception.

Q: Scott, what first attracted you to speculation?

SCOTT: I would like to say that it was probably my interest in puzzles and in problem solving. It was a fascination trying to figure out how to get an answer and how to compete at a certain level. I'd be lying to say there wasn't a financial interest as well. Clearly, people who have done well in speculation have reaped significant material rewards.

Q: Was it competing against others or competing against yourself?

SCOTT: Oh, I'd say definitely against myself initially. My childhood hobbies and interests in things like juggling, unicycle riding, and magic were all personal challenges. Speculation seemed to me the ultimate personal challenge: you are competing against yourself and there is no do-over. It's for keeps! If you win you get to keep your winnings and if you lose you have to face up to what's going wrong immediately. I find that to be a motivating factor. Trading is not like a card game that you can walk away from at any time. If a trade is not going well, you can't walk away from it! You're forced to face it and yourself and take action. I find that to be a very strong motivational force. I need something like that to push me. I was your classic underachiever. I need something like that to get me into gear. I used to wait until the last minute to write term papers, or I'd wait until the last minute to study for a big test. I need to feel the pressure.

Q: But I bet you still did well on the test.

SCOTT: Yes, I did reasonably well. But I crave the pressure. I find the market seems to give me that push.

Q: In the market you get that push every day. Is that what you mean, Scott?

SCOTT: Yes, for me, it's highly motivational. Selecting a mutual fund for me is not highly motivational, to identify the best mutual fund over the next five to ten years. Although there might be an element of challenge involved, there's no sense of immediate gratification for me. As I look at the market I try to determine my next step in the process. I look for the next piece of the puzzle that will allow me to accomplish my trading goals.

Q: Do you believe what first interested you in trading still holds the same attraction?

SCOTT: Definitely. However, it has elevated itself from being pure speculation to a combination of speculation and running a capital management business. And when you tie those two together, it becomes an entirely different animal.

Q: In what way?

SCOTT: When you're managing money on the institutional level, you're not simply trying to quantify your own appetite for risk. It is not about what you can tolerate and what you think is a proper return. In effect, you're packaging yourself as an asset class and trying to see how you fit in a larger portfolio of stocks, bonds, derivatives, and currency overlays. Therefore, it is important that your trading results have a certain profile that will enable your product to have a fit within a larger scheme of things. You must take into consideration your daily standard deviations and sharp ratio, as well as your average rate of return and maximum drawdown.

As a discretionary trader, I didn't look at any of those things for determining what position size I would take or how long I would hold a trade; not even how much pain I was going to take on a trade. It worked out to be simply a decision based on a trade-by-trade basis and how strongly I felt, or how much I felt the market fundamentals or technicals come into play.

As a money manager, though, some of the same overriding principles are still true. You're trying to gain an edge, to exploit an advantage. But the institutional framework is distinctly different, and for many traders the transition is very difficult. There are great traders who are not able to make the change, traders that are much better traders than I could ever be. But the world of the discretionary trader and the money manager are two entirely separate worlds.

Q: Scott, specifically, why is it so hard for many exceptional floor traders to make it in an institutional setting?

SCOTT: I think many discretionary traders, because of their strong tolerance for risk, trade in a way that is impossible in the institutional setting. Many times for successful floor traders their return at the end of the year has come about due to perhaps a handful of trades where they doubled or tripled or quadrupled their position size and captured a good two- or three-day move in the market, resulting in substantial winnings. Most of the other time they're just winning and losing, in due course. The point is that the bulk of their year is coming about through a handful of well-positioned trades where they are willing to expand their risk. This was my own experience as well. I would step up a couple of my personal trades in any given year very strongly. And it was finding a time and trading around until that opportunity presented itself—the skill was knowing when to take the rubber band off the bankroll and push a position. You can't do that in institutional trading. You may occasionally be able to push a position a little bit harder, and from time to time you hear stories of some hedge fund managers who parlayed positions tremendously, but even then you're talking about maybe a little stronger than what they normally would do; significantly more than what you might do on your own.

In the institutional setting you're trying to create a product that your client wants for his overall portfolio, as well as providing decent returns. When it's for yourself, you're simply looking for returns, plain and simple. At the end of the year, all that matters is how much money you've accumulated. As I said, in the management world that's not the main issue. You're expected to make money because you're a professional. It's the profile of the returns that is all-important.

Q: The quality of the return, is that correct?

SCOTT: Yes, very much so. Not only the consistency of the returns but the correlation. If you earn money at the exact same time that the S&P earns money for a passive long, or if you earn money at the exact same time that another fund manager does, you're going to be less in demand. So again it's creating a different product. But having said all of this, I do think that how you take advantage of market conditions and how you view risk is going to play a big role in how you ultimately perform. I think, frankly, many discretionary traders would be very unhappy, even bored, doing what we do. I mean, we grind it out, you know, 30, 40, 50 basis points a day.

Q: Scott, what do you think are some of the psychological biases that make trading so difficult for most people?

SCOTT: Traders tend to do irrational things. They'll take greater risks simply to avoid realizing a loss in the face of statistics that inform them to do otherwise. That probably is one of the most prominent psychological pitfalls that traders fall victim to.

Q: Selective denial.

SCOTT: Sure. If you know you have a certain distribution of your profits and losses, and you break your rules to hold on to the position longer, you realize how you're skewing it; you skew it so greatly by doubling or tripling the position size if it's outside your perimeter, and more so than just simply tinkering with your profile. It causes not only the statistics to work against you, but it causes your judgment to be greatly impaired. Also, when you speak to a trader who is experiencing a drawdown, sometimes you're just amazed at some of the things that they say. They're in another world. I mean, I've been there, and I've had people say to me, "You know, when I was talking to you during this period you weren't making any sense. What were you thinking of?" So I think that kind of unnatural or "magical" thinking is probably the greatest danger; also, getting yourself in a negative zone where you are in a state of denial, in which you lose touch with your trading objectives. Sometimes people even develop a paranoia that somehow the market is out to get them, that traders are running stops, and it all becomes a very personal and irrational thing.

Q: You lose your sense of discipline and find yourself engaged in an irrational perspective where you feel as though you are a psychological victim to market forces.

SCOTT: I think this idea about selective memory is crucial, because we see a lot of negative reinforcement. You tend to trade what worked best the last time, and if you broke the rules last time and it worked—you overstayed your position while in a huge drawdown but then the position snapped back—there is reinforcement to do the same thing again. I have a friend who's an S&P trader, and he had three spectacular months in a row. He is a serious student of the psychology of trading. He can espouse all the rules, and he is very focused on his trading. Unfortunately, I just heard from him recently that in the last couple of months he had really gotten hurt. He began to list for me all the things that he had done. It was a classic example of getting caught up in the emotion of a market. He told me all the different rules that he broke. I just could not believe it, and he himself couldn't believe in retrospect that he would do all these things. He would pull the stop out of the market and let the position go. He would double up. In short, he made all the trading errors that he had told himself he wasn't going to do. Maybe it was because of all the euphoria of winning.

Q: The interesting thing, and I think this gets down to the whole issue of risk, is that how we as traders define and then adopt risk is more of a psychological or emotional response than a cognitive decision. You can ask a lot of traders what the rules are, and they'll know them; even so, they'll violate the rules in an effort to rationalize to themselves that they're not wrong or that they don't have to take the loss.

SCOTT: Yes, it is very interesting.

Q: Scott, what personal prejudices or biases do you believe you had to wrestle with in order to effect a successful result in your own trading?

SCOTT: I think for me it was trying to differentiate between being and making money; realizing that I could take my ego out of it and be willing to take a quick loss; in other words, to manage the risk on the position rather than having my ego say "I know I'm right on the position." I was able to resolve this issue successfully when I understood that the risk management side of my trading had to take precedence over the ego side. The reason was simple: because the risk side of it was the only way that I could stay in the game.

Q: How do you deal with the issue of uncertainty?

SCOTT: As you know, my background is in philosophy; however, initially, I didn't see the connection between philosophy and trading. But as I wrestled with some ups and downs in my trading, I tried to figure out a way to attain greater certainty to boost my confidence. I began to realize that some of my philosophical training in logic about universal and particular claims had application to my understanding and operation in the markets. If you have four or five trades that have worked in the past, it does not imply that this trade is going to work in the present because you cannot have all the data points, you cannot have a bank of all the trades ever completed or all the data points of a price chart back to the beginning of time. In a philosophical sense, then, there's no way to have that complete certainty. Once I was able to come to grips with the reality that there was no Holy Grail, I began to realize that trading was prime ground for probability and statistics. This was a startling revelation for me. It provided the impetus for a shift in my own trading from purely discretionary seat-of-the-pants-type trading to a more systematic approach based on probabilities and number crunching.

Q: In terms of this philosophical shift, Scott, how did you handle the issue of certainty in terms of circumscribing risk?

SCOTT: Well, the main issue for me was simply making sure I could stay in business, because I had a few brushes with death right out of the gates.

Q: You mean financial death.

SCOTT: Right. But it had to happen to me several times before I was cured—you know, realizing that although the leverage is great, you're always given enough rope to hang yourself. And if you're not careful, you will. One time I had these bear spreads on. They went against me but I put more on. When they went further against me I put even more on. The next thing I knew I was down 70 percent on my trading account. I was sweating bullets, not knowing what I was going to do, and thinking, this is like déjà vu! I said to myself, "Didn't I just do this three months ago in the coffee position?"

Q: Yes, it's like déjà vu all over again except you don't remember what to do.

SCOTT: Exactly. And when the position came back, finally, I was out of most of the position. The pain was excruciating, and I couldn't hang on. It was totally debilitating. I was mentally and physically exhausted. Just after I got out I believe the spread position worked for about 17 trading days in a row.

Q: What did you learn from that experience?

SCOTT: I learned that something was going to have to change in my trading. But a couple of months later I got caught in the soybean squeeze before the Board of Trade forced Firuzzi to liquidate. I had a large position and did the same thing all over again. I was pushed out the day before the board started making them liquidate. And of course the thing collapsed, and I would have made another great deal of money. During this entire time I realized that I was flirting with disaster. Extremes moved farther than I had expected; the leverage allowed me to force the risk, and emotionally it was gut-wrenching to place myself in these situations. I said, "There's got to be a better way." This was when I started to realize the importance of probabilities in managing risk, and I began to do research in order to study systematic ways to test different trading ideas. But I probably wouldn't have done that if I hadn't had my hand burned in the fire. The pain made me realize there was another, more effective way.

I think many traders go through this cycle early on, where there is some skill and some randomness to their trading. Then there is the crucial time period where they either learn how to manage the risk or they end up giving it all back. I think I was kind of at a plateau where I had learned to do a few things well, but I was constantly pushing the envelope and flirting with disaster. Of course, I was fortunate that I didn't get knocked out of the game entirely before I began to learn to manage the risk better.

I think in the beginning, when I had less to lose, I was willing to risk more personally. I started trading with borrowed money. I couldn't afford to lose that, yet I took risks that I would never in a million years consider taking now. My appetite for risk has changed every single year that I've been a trader, and I'm always moving to a more conservative approach. Today I have a lot more respect for just how extreme extremes can get. Consider in the last ten-year time period, we've had the stock market crash, the Gulf War, the fall of communism: all things that if you would have tried to figure out the odds of you probably never would have given any of them much of a chance. Maybe having a family, starting to have children, played a role in my development as a trader. Or perhaps, seeing other traders suffering significant financial pain has influenced me to be more risk averse.

Q: Scott, how do you currently calculate risk?

SCOTT: We look at risk on a portfolio level as well as an individual market level. And we look at risk from expectations based on recent volatility and the worst-case scenario. If we see extreme price action in a variety of different markets, then we know that we're going to be incorporating that data into our trading model, in addition to some specific tricks of the trade that look-see beyond the pure numbers. For example, volatility may drop to such a low level that the model thinks that you're only risking ten basis points on a particular trade. And to risk ten basis points, that may mean you need to put on, say, a thousand contracts. But because volatility is so low, you know from being a real-time trader that high volatility follows low volatility and that suddenly volatility may pick up. If something happened, particularly while the market that you're in is closed, it could result in a significant price gap. But the model itself can't see that type of risk, so we've added certain proprietary limits to our models. So even though they think that the risk is a lot lower, we know realistically the risk is not.

Q: Scott, what do you think is the riskiest thing you ever did or experienced in your life?

SCOTT: The riskiest thing for me was to stick with trading. I thought to myself, if I quit, then what? Especially in the beginning, I just kept thinking about how I was going to make good on my losses and support my family. For me the risk was the full-time commitment to be a trader.

I see a lot of part-time traders, a lot of people that have a job and trade on the side. They say to themselves, "If I ever get good enough at trading, I'll quit my day job." The risk for me was to make the decision wholeheartedly to go for it. I just told myself, "I will always be a trader. Failure is not an option."

Q: So the riskiest thing that you ever did was make the commitment to deal with the risk?

SCOTT: Yes, to live with it. I think when it comes right down to it, a lot of traders who haven't really succeeded are afraid to fully commit. It requires total focus. If you want to be a brain surgeon your commitment and focus must be complete. You don't go into med school thinking, maybe I'll do this part-time.

Q: I guess most people don't think about that aspect of risk.

SCOTT: Right. It's like the opportunity lost in not taking the trade.

Q: That's a huge risk.

SCOTT: Exactly. Any successful trader will tell about the pain of not being in the trade. Everybody's got a few stories. The last time I had that experience was in the first quarter of 1995 when the dollar collapsed and I never got into the trade. That was painful. The risk of not being there, the loss of the opportunity, I believe, is probably the most downplayed of all the risks out there.

Q: Have you ever attempted to quantify that kind of risk?

SCOTT: We've run studies on our trading, and I know many other traders have too. If you didn't participate in one or two of your best days every year, it would significantly affect your average. When you start looking and quantifying that way, you realize that you've got to be there digging it out day after day. When you're playing the odds, you can't take a break.

Q: Somebody showed me a study with regard to the Dow. If you subtract seven or eight core days, the Dow since the inception of the bull market in 1982 is basically flat. If you weren't invested in these seven or eight days, you wouldn't have any return.

SCOTT: So for us, the opportunity lost, the risk of not being there, is huge for what we do currently, but that's because there's such a high reliance on the numbers. When I was a pure discretionary trader, if I had an opportunity lost, I just doubled up on the next trade. You could sit and be patient and wait for the next wave. Because as I said before, all you care about is net returns. When I first started working for a large trading firm as a trader, I was giving advice about the grain markets and how we could enhance our systematic grain trading through my understanding of the fundamentals, the probabilities, and so forth. And there was a day in July when the beans were limit up. They had just broken a key level, and the funds were piling on; it was a Friday. We had limit positions on and I recommended—there was about a half hour left in trading—that we get out. The weather patterns were changing. It looked to me that the market could open limit down on the following Monday. I said to the senior trader, "We should liquidate." And he said, "I agree with you 100 percent, but we have to stay in this position." And I said, "What do you mean?" His response was, "You have to understand that the risk for me is not the loss on the trade; the risk for me is if something changes in the weather pattern over the weekend, and the market opens limit up for the next three days. All my competition have long positions and will be making money, and I won't be there. If it opens limit down, and we're all in the same boat, I'm not penalized for that!" It was a very illuminating experience for me to realize that somebody was making a trading decision based upon that kind of thinking.

Q: It's like being keyed to the index.

SCOTT: Exactly. The risk of not being there was greater than the risk of taking the loss. Fortunately, for the style of trading that we do and what institutions expect from Dominion Capital, we're so noncorrelated to everybody else that there is no real benchmark for us other than that we tend to be strongly negatively correlated to the trend players. So, if the trend is rolling over, it's very important that we're involved because we're expected to be a short-term hedge against those types of moves.

Q: Scott, once you felt as though you had a better grasp of the whole issue of risk, do you feel it positively affected your motivation for trading?

SCOTT: I think the confidence level and the motivation level have been high all the way through. However, as I reflect back on my trading, I think that my confidence is much more solid than it was. I think early on I had some false confidence, and I think that through some sheer randomness I avoided self-destructing. Looking back, I did things, managed portfolios, in ways that were not prudent and were inviting disaster. But I was confident at the time that I was doing the right thing. I think the confidence I have today is much more solid because it is based on hard research, a statistical understanding of price action. I'm confident now in the sense that I know risk can be managed. You can't control the upside, but you can manage the risk. We can adjust to changes in volatility so that we have consistent risk on every trade. In general, we want to risk approximately 30 basis points on a full position. Our trading models give me a tremendous amount of confidence.

Q: You profile each trade to exhibit a risk of 30 basis points, or are you talking about the entire portfolio?

SCOTT: Each trade. And then that gives us a portfolio profile as well, what we should expect as the daily standard deviation. About 50 percent of our trades are profitable. Our winners are twice the size of our losses. We trade about two to three times per market per month, and so on a 50 percent system, the distribution is somewhat like flipping a coin. And in a perfect world, flipping a coin is going to be heads, tails, heads, tails, heads, tails. However, in the real world, it is more like . . .

Q: . . . heads, heads, heads, heads, heads, heads, tails.

SCOTT: Right. You get runs. And the most predominant runs we get are in twos and threes. So it goes, heads, heads, tails, tails, tails, and so forth. The same is true of our trading. The norm is to get runs of two and three wins or losses in a row. So for us to lose two or three times in a row in any one market is not unusual; it's the norm. What happened to us in one particular month was that we had two or three losses in individual markets across the whole portfolio. Now, what did that tell us about our trading? Well, we expected it, and as a matter of fact, many of our clients who were in tune with what we're trying to accomplish statistically were willing to step up to the plate and actually buy the drawdown to play the mean reversion to our fiscal mean. And sure enough, we doubled our assets over the next couple of months. For the next few months we had rip-roaring perfor-mance. I mean, we came out of the gates very strong.

Q: When it came to understanding risk, what did you learn most about yourself?

SCOTT: In retrospect, I'm a little surprised that I've been as willing to assume as much risk as I have in the past. But I don't think that's unusual for traders. I think most traders, if they re-view their pasts, at times wonder what really makes them tick. What kind of animal am I that I'm willing to take on so much un-certainty? Particularly when you talk to people outside the busi-ness of speculation, who have their money wrapped up in CDs. They're concerned about a quarter of a point interest rate or they're thinking about dividends on utility stocks. I realize that I'm operating in a completely different cosmos, not any better or worse, but just different.

Q: Maybe slightly less rational.

SCOTT: Perhaps, but you know, the entrepreneurial side of me looks back and says nothing substantial in the business or fi-nancial world has ever been gained without the use of leverage. From my perspective, the key is to be philosophical and scien-tific and recognize that the leverage has to be controlled by you so that you're not controlled by it.

I also learned that I enjoy taking on the risk and I like it. I'm trying to gain satisfaction from the business side of what I do, as well as from the trading side. But it's a different type of satisfac-tion. The adrenaline rush that you may get from holding a hun-dred contracts in your personal account when the market is limit up is completely different, but knowing that you have one of the best sharp ratios over the last three years is still a great ac-complishment.

12

Risk versus Reward

Almost every person I interviewed felt that money management was even more important than the trading method. Many potentially successful systems on trading approaches have led to disaster because the trader applying the strategy lacked a method of controlling risk.

—*Jack Schwager,* The New Market Wizards

The following list takes into consideration the previous discussion of risk as well as the interviews with top traders as they relate specifically to applying risk/reward considerations to trading markets.

Principles of Successful Risk Taking

- Define your loss.
- Believe in yourself and unlimited market possibilities.
- Have a well-defined money management program.
- Don't buy price.
- Don't take tips.
- Don't trade angry or euphoric.
- Trade aggressively at your numbers and points.
- Focus on opportunities.

- Consistently apply your day trading system.
- Be highly motivated.
- Don't overtrade.
- Never average a loss.
- Take small losses, big profits.
- Have no bias to either side of the market.
- Preserve capital.
- Think in probabilities.
- Always trade in a highly positive and resourceful state of mind.
- Act in certainty.
- The market is never wrong.

The key point here is that successful trading is a direct result of a well-disciplined approach of calculated risk taking that once again takes the following points into consideration.

- Trader effectively manages emotion.
- Trader is aware of overcoming the pitfalls of crowd psychology.
- Trader understands his or her conscious and unconscious motivations.
- Trader risks an appropriate percentage of the overall portfolio.
- Trader acknowledges personal abilities and limitations.
- Trader is systematic and consistent in approach.
- Trader stays emotionally balanced during winning and losing periods.
- Trader resists trades that are outside a defined risk parameter.
- Trader is open to calculated risk opportunities.
- Trader is analytical and disciplined in every stage of the investment process.

As you read over each item in the list of principles of successful risk taking, ask yourself the following questions:

- How does all this relate to me?
- How do I personally experience risk?
- What physical symptoms do I experience?
- What emotions do I have when taking risk in the market?
- What do I hear in my mind's ear?
- What sensory imagery do I experience?
- What specific anxieties do I have of a recurring kind?
- What am I thinking when I take a loss?
- What do I believe about myself and the market when taking a loss?
- What self-defeating attitudes do I possess that I can overcome?
- How can I incorporate all of these principles into my current trading system?

Bottom Line

As you consider your responses to the questions above, consider the beliefs held in common by the top traders.

Positive Beliefs of the Top Traders

- I believe I am or will be a successful trader.
- I believe I can achieve excellent results in my trading.
- I believe I can identify and execute winning trades.
- I believe I can trade with confidence.
- I believe I can trade effortlessly and automatically.
- I believe each day's performance is fresh.
- I believe I am personally responsible for all my trading results.
- I believe I can be successful without being perfect.
- I believe my performance as a trader does not reflect on my self-worth.
- I believe one bad trade is just that.
- I believe trading is a process.

- I believe that by believing in myself and in any proven methodology and by approaching trading each day with a fresh, positive state of mind I possess the ultimate trading edge.

Trading is a rewarding universe of unlimited possibilities when approached with maturity and well-managed risk. It is intellectually challenging and affords independently minded individuals the ability to participate in a personally fulfilling and profitable activity. The key to successful trading is always the same: turning a potentially risky situation into an undertaking of carefully planned, systematic, and well-calculated risk management.

Success in trading!

For Further Reading

Abell, Howard. *The Day Trader's Advantage.* Chicago: Dearborn, 1996.

Abell, Howard. *Spread Trading.* Chicago: Dearborn, 1997.

Barach, Roland. *Mindtraps: Mastering the Inner World of Investing.* Homewood: Dow Jones-Irwin, 1988.

Baruch, Bernard M. *Baruch: My Own Story.* New York: Holt, Rinehart & Winston, 1957.

Bernstein, Peter. *Against the Gods: The Remarkable Story of Risk.* New York: John Wiley & Sons, 1996.

Douglas, Mark. *The Disciplined Trader.* New York: New York Institute of Finance, 1990.

Gann, W.D. *How to Make Profits Trading in Commodities.* Pomeroy: Lambert-Gann, 1976.

Koppel, Robert. *The Tao of Trading.* Chicago: Dearborn, 1998.

Koppel, Robert. *Bulls, Bears, and Millionaires.* Chicago: Dearborn, 1997.

Koppel, Robert. *The Intuitive Trader: Developing Your Inner Market Wisdom.* New York: John Wiley & Sons, 1996.

Koppel, Robert and Abell, Howard. *The Innergame of Trading: Modeling the Psychology of the Top Traders.* New York: McGraw-Hill, 1993.

Koppel, Robert and Abell, Howard. *The Outer Game of Trading: Modeling the Trading Strategies of Today's Market Wizards.* New York: McGraw-Hill, 1994.

Le Bon, Gustave. *The Crowd: A Study of the Popular Mind.* Atlanta: Cherokee, 1982 (2nd ed.).

Plummer, Tony. *The Psychology of Technical Analysis.* New York: McGraw-Hill, 1994.

Schwager, Jack D. *Market Wizards: Interviews with Top Traders.* New York: New York Institute of Finance, 1989.

Schwager, Jack D. *The New Market Wizards: Conversations with America's Top Traders.* New York: HarperBusiness, 1992.

Sperandeo, Victor with Brown, T. Sullivan. *Trader Vic—Methods of a Wall Street Master.* New York: John Wiley & Sons, 1991.

Index

About the Author

Howard Abell is Chief Operating Officer of the Innergame Division of Rand Financial Services, Inc., concentrating on brokerage and execution services for institutional and professional traders. Rand Financial Services is a Chicago-based futures clearing merchant (FCM) clearing all major world exchanges. Abell is the coauthor, with Bob Koppel, of *The Innergame of Trading* (Irwin, 1993) and *The Outer Game of Trading* (Irwin, 1994). He is the author of *The Day Trader's Advantage* (Dearborn, 1996) and *Spread Trading* (Dearborn, 1997). Abell currently manages Tao Partners, a Commodity Trading Advisor.

For additional information about Rand Financial Services or Tao Partners, please contact:

Innergame Div./Rand Financial Services, Inc.
Chicago Mercantile Exchange
30 South Wacker Drive
Suite 2200
Chicago, IL 60606
312-559-8898
800-726-3088
Fax: 312-559-8848
e-mail: hma@innergame.com
Visit our Web site at www.innergame.com